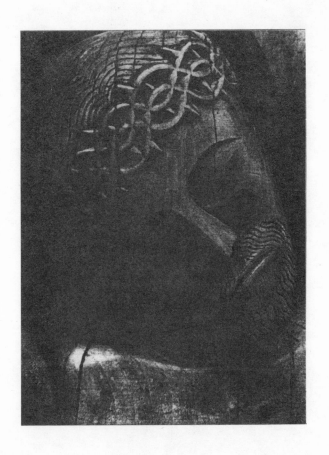

Gérard Rossé

The Cry of Jesus
on the Cross

A Biblical and Theological Study

Translated by
Stephen Wentworth Arndt

Paulist Press
New York / Mahwah

Cover art: Detail of altarpiece, American folk art, Norwegian-American Museum, Decorah, Iowa. Photo © by Gene Plaisted. Cover design by A. Victor Schwarz.

Originally published as *Il Grido Di Gesù in Croce* copyright by Citta' Nuova Editrice, Rome. English translation 1987 by The Missionary Society of St. Paul the Apostle in the State of New York.

Book design by Nighthawk Design.

Library of Congress Cataloging-in-Publication Data

Rossé, Gérard.
   [Grido di Gesù in croce. English]
   The cry of Jesus on the cross: a biblical and theological study/
Gérard Rossé; translated by Stephen W. Arndt.
     p. cm.
   Translation of: Il grido di Gesù in croce.
   Bibliography: p.
   ISBN 0-8091-2922-1 (pbk.): $8.95 (est.)
   1. Jesus Christ—Seven last words. 2. Bible. N.T. Mark XV, 34—
Criticism, interpretation, etc. 3. Bible. N.T. Matthew XXVII,
46—Criticism, interpretation, etc. 4. Jesus Christ—Person and
offices. I. Title.
BT456.R6713 1987   87-27392
232.9′635—dc19   CIP

Published by Paulist Press
997 Macarthur Boulevard
Mahwah, New Jersey 07430

Printed and bound in the
United States of America

Contents

Preface

The cry of Jesus on the cross—"My God, my God, why have you forsaken me?"—has always given rise to interest and perplexity in Christian thought.

It seems to me—and I am not only thinking of J. Moltmann's book *The Crucified God*—that today in particular this subject has received a new topical interest. Numerous articles and studies have been dedicated to it. I have thus considered it opportune to present to the non-specialized reader a synthesis that will permit him to have a total view of this theme.

Certainly, in the course of the centuries, the abandonment experienced by Christ on the cross has nourished the reflection of numerous Christian thinkers and fathers of spirituality, such as the Rhineland mystics, who have known how to find in this cry a content capable of helping them on the road toward God. But Jesus' cry of abandonment has above all caused questions, dismay, even scandal. A certain fear is noticeable, whether one avoids speaking of this subject or whether one primarily examines it in order to integrate the reality of the abandonment into the faith and traditional Christology.

St. Augustine has recourse to a sort of *communicatio idiomatum,* of an exchange of properties, between Christ and the Church: "Why, then, do we disdain hearing the voice of the body from the mouth of the head? When he suffered for the Church, it was the Church that suffered in him, just as when the Church suffered for him, it was he who suffered with the Church. As we have heard the voice of the Church which suffered in Christ: 'My God, my God, turn to me your face; why have you abandoned me?' so have we also heard the voice of Christ who suffered in the Church: 'Saul, Saul, why are you persecuting me?' " (Epist 140, 18). The Bishop of Hippo knows how to exploit the rule of Tyconius wonderfully well in order to overcome the problem.

In practice, Scholasticism distinguished two spheres in the soul of the Savior, and thus it was able to explain how Christ could experience abandonment and beatific joy at the same time. This was to become the thought of classical theology until recent times. But it does not seem to be an exhaustive explanation. Even today, there is a temptation to empty the cry of abandonment of its content by drowning it in the optimism expressed in the conclusion of Psalm 22.

But the times are changing. In current Christian movements such as the "movimento dei focolari," the reality of the abandoned Jesus is a fundamental point of spirituality, and for many believers it has become the key to behavior in personal and community life as well as in relations with the world.

Even among theologians the perspective has evolved. The problem is no longer so much one of harmonizing the cry as well as possible with what the faith teaches about Christ and his unique relationship to the Father as it is one of discovering the true revelational value that such a cry manifests. It is not essentially a question of saving a certain Christology but of taking the abandonment of Christ seriously. Moltmann is no longer the only one to express the conviction that in the mouth of the crucified Jesus Psalm 22:2 constitutes a crucial turning point for the whole of theological thought.

Evidently, the text that relates the cry of abandonment can no longer be considered as a report that would have the purpose of informing the Christian about one of the many utterances that Jesus was able to make on the cross.

Through its various exponents, contemporary theology is becoming ever more conscious of the enormous charge of revelation this text contains and that only its integration into a sufficiently broad theology of redemption (which opens onto the mystery of the Trinity itself) will be able to do it justice. There is, of course, still much to do.

The views of some Fathers will become topical again, especially those of the Greeks, such as Gregory of Nyssa or Cyril of Alexandria, which are synthesized in formulae such as "God became man so that man might become God" or "Only that which has been assumed has been saved."

Today, the Gospel text can no longer be approached and studied as in the past. Modern exegesis has refined its instruments. It requires a new viewpoint and a new mentality in order to penetrate the written datum. It likewise allows one to look at the text from a more correct point of view and avoids letting one be locked into psychological considerations or stopping at a purely historicizing reading which sees the text as a chronicle of what has happened and no more.

That certainly does not mean that the opinions of the exegetes are now in accord concerning the interpretation of the cry. But some lines of convergence do appear. One is trying to understand this cry without isolating it from its context, in the dimension it receives from the Old Testament, in its theological meaning, etc.

The historical question is inevitably posed: Did Jesus really utter these words on the cross?

If one knows the nature of the Gospel text, the answer to this question is no longer so simple. In order not to disorient the reader unfamiliar with the field, I have thought it fitting to present by way of introduction a brief historical panorama of how one has arrived in exegesis at the current way of reading a Gospel text.

If attention should be directed above all to the theological interpretation of the cry of abandonment, if moreover the exegete has no possibility of peremptorily affirming its historicity, this theological interpretation must nevertheless rest on what is real. It must find roots in history and in the life of Jesus if it does not want to be gratuitous and thus empty. These data are incontestable: there is the historical fact of the death of Jesus on the cross, and that means on the wood of the curse. It is precisely this death that the cry interprets, and thus it should be taken with all possible seriousness. The continuity in this regard with the thought of the apostle Paul on the crucified Jesus and the scandal of the cross is surprising.

Another important historical datum is the life and behavior of Jesus himself: his unique relationship with the Father, his complete obedience, and his way of facing his passion and death. In the light of the existence of Jesus, the cry of abandonment reveals and expresses the summit of his unity with the Father.

Finally, let us not forget the resurrection itself as the Father's response. It confirms everything.

The reader should approach the text confidently, examine it in the most simple way possible from the exegetical point of view, grasp its position within the context, and penetrate beyond the redactional level to the earliest tradition. After having studied the historical problem, he will be able to grasp the various meanings that this cry acquires in the mouth of the Suffering Servant, the Messiah, and the Son of God. And in this way he will arrive at the understanding contained in the present Gospel of Mark.

A historical panorama will lead us to the various contemporary interpretations before opening the cry up to a fuller reflection on God's love for man and on the trinitarian life that this interpretation of the death of Christ reveals.

The Question of the Historical Jesus and of the Christ of Faith, or How To Read the Gospel Text[1]

In Search of the Historical Jesus (the Nineteenth Century)

Before approaching our topic true and proper—the cry of abandonment of the crucified Jesus in Mark 15:34 (Mt 27:46)—it seems useful to me to introduce the reader, who is often not abreast of the new knowledge in the biblical field and thus accustomed to a historicizing or moralizing reading of the Gospel, to the understanding of the Gospel text.

For many centuries it was accepted that the things written in the Gospels happened just as they are related. It was natural to read the passion of Jesus as if it were a report, a chronicle of events, and thus to hold that what is written there constitutes an exact description of what took place historically. But this notion was weakened and then finally collapsed when at the end of the eighteenth century the Gospels were no longer considered solely as inspired books—infallible and untouchable—but also as historical documents, thus as books that can be analyzed and studied critically just like other works of antiquity.

The historical-critical method was being refined. One discovered the existence of documents or sources underlying our Gospels. By reaching more ancient sources of which the evangelists had made use—sources closer to the historical Jesus—one

1

thought oneself to have finally arrived at an historical portrait of Jesus, one liberated from the dogmatic image that had covered it up; one thought oneself to have rediscovered his personality, his original teaching, the facts of his life, how he really lived, and thus a portrait detached from the interpretation the sacred author himself had made of it in his work.

The investigation lasted for more than a century, up until the beginnings of our own. The result was not exactly satisfying. In the effort to restore the authentic figure of Jesus of Nazareth to light, there emerged many *Lives of Jesus* in which the latter appeared as the arbitrary product of the times in which these works were written: there was the romantic Jesus, the "sweet Galilean dreamer" of Renan, but also the liberal Jesus, the socialist Jesus, etc.

Without intending to do so, one arrived at precisely the contrary result: the most ancient Gospel—that of Mark—and the most primitive traditions contained in the Gospels are already a *theological work* and not an historical document about Jesus. One began to discern the true literary genre of those original writings called Gospels. They neither are, it was said, nor do they wish to be purely historical documents in any of their parts but are already testimonies of faith, i.e., a Christian interpretation of the deeds and words of Jesus in the light of the post-Easter faith. The Gospel sources are therefore not in a position to help us reconstruct the history of Jesus as it is usually understood, namely, as an objective report and the chronological succession of events.

The road that leads to the historical Jesus seemed closed. In 1906 the Alsatian theologian Albert Schweitzer—better known for his work as a physician in Africa and for the Nobel peace prize in 1952—delivered the "funeral oration" of this entire period of research on the life of Jesus in a book that has become a classic: *Die Geschichte der Leben-Jesu-Forschung* (*History of the Life of Jesus Research*—the title dates back to the 1913 edition). He writes: "Things have gone rather strangely for the Life of Jesus Research. It set out to find the historical Jesus and thought it could transfer him as he was, i.e., as teacher and savior, into our times. It loosened the bonds with which he had been chained for

centuries to the rocks of Church doctrine and rejoiced when life
and movement returned to this figure again and they saw the historical man, Jesus, approach them. But he did not remain; rather
he passed our times over and returned to his own" (pp. 631ff).
The exegetes thought that they could sketch the genuine face of
the historical Jesus. In reality, they constructed a Christ who mir-
rored the demands and the culture of their age. The true Jesus fled
these attempts and "returned to his own times."

Bultmann

After the First World War, R. Bultmann, professor at Marburg, friend and colleague of Heidegger, carried the result of the
Jesus research to extreme consequences: seeing that the Gospels
do not recount the history of Jesus and do not make his personality known but testify to the faith of the primitive Church, this
faith should suffice. It is in it and only in it that the Word of God
interpellates me and solicits me. This Word does not require any
kind of legitimation; it needs no support in history in order to be
believed. Thus, it does not matter who the historical Jesus was.[2]

For the believer, therefore, only the Christ believed and announced in the kerygma has value, i.e., in the Christian preaching
of the apostolic Church, not the teaching or behavior of the historical Jesus. The Jesus of history, his person, and his teaching
belong to Judaism, not to the Church; he therefore does not have
a normative value. The Christian kerygma, and thus the faith, has
its origin in the death and resurrection of Jesus (the latter being
understood as an interpretation of the death): it alone—and not
the historical Jesus—has salvific value. Bultmann sythesizes all of
this on the first page of his *Theology of the New Testament*,
which appeared in 1953: "The message of Jesus belongs to the
presuppositions of the theology of the New Testament but is not
a part of this theology itself."

A real fissure has thus been created between the historical Jesus
and the Christ of faith announced in the Church. According to
Bultmann, it is only the latter who counts for the believer of today
because God speaks to us in the kerygma.

How Does Bultmann See Jesus' Cry of Abandonment?

In his important work *Geschichte der synoptischen Tradition* (*History of the Synoptic Tradition*),[3] he writes: "The cry of Jesus in Mk 15:34 (elôi ktl.) is probably a secondary interpretation of Mk 15:37 where the simple fact of a loud cry is narrated" (p. 342).

Bultmann thus considers the inarticulate cry related in Mark 15:37 as the earlier: "Then Jesus, uttering a loud cry, breathed his last." Afterward, the Christian community would have "interpreted" this cry with the help of the initial verse of Psalm 22: "My God, my God, why have you abandoned me?"

Given the fact that the Gospels—and thus the passion narrative also—are not intended as a chronicle account of the events, the hypothesis of Bultmann is tenable, even if it is only a hypothesis. A problem, however, remains: Is it essential for the Christian community that this interpretation have a foundation in reality or not? Is it important whether the historical Jesus actually experienced what Psalm 22 expresses?

Bultmann would respond that the historicity of the articulate cry is without importance for faith and that the experience of Psalm 22:2 on the part of the Crucified is in any case secondary since this faith should rest solely on the Word of God that I encounter in the kerygma without seeking a legitimation in the facts.

The Research after Bultmann

In short, Bultmann has radicalized the Protestant dogma of *sola fides,* i.e., of a faith that does not seek security in history. As an inevitable consequence, the position of the Marburg theologian has evoked a contrary reaction in both Protestant and Catholic camps.

Attention is now being directed to Jesus of Nazareth in a new way. One is reflecting on his importance for faith, on the relation between faith and history, etc. It is not surprising that the criticism provoked by Bultmann's conception has also come precisely from his own disciples. The beginning was made in 1953 by a lecture of Käsemann on the "problem of the historical Jesus." This exegete recalled that the faith of the primitive Church—as the writings of the New Testament testify—never separated the historical Jesus from the Christ it believed and announced and that it always defended and maintained the identity of the Jesus of history with the Risen Lord against every tendency to divide them or to privilege one aspect to the detriment of the other. "Clearly it (the primitive Church) is of the opinion that one can understand the earthly Jesus only in terms of Easter and thus in his dignity as Lord of the community and that vice versa one is not able to understand Easter adequately if one abstracts from the earthly Jesus."[4]

The reality of the earthly Jesus thus occupies an important position, and the renewed interest of the post-Bultmannian period in its regard is not secondary, simply to satisfy the curiosity of the historian, but legitimate and necessary, even doctrinal. The New Testament writings allow us to see that the understanding of Christ on the part of the apostolic Church was pluralistic from the very beginning but, as Käsemann again writes, "One was in accord in judging that the history of Jesus was constitutive for faith because the earthly Jesus and the exalted Lord are identical. The Easter faith grounded the Christian kerygma, but it did not give it its first and exclusive content" (p. 203).

The historical Jesus is thus not only an introduction to the kerygma. Rather, he belongs there by right; he constitutes its criterion and, to a large extent, its content. Without him, faith would be emptied of all meaning.[5]

A kerygma devoid of interest in the pre-Easter Jesus has never existed. The chasm between Christ and Jesus cannot be justified, and the wish to absolutize the first to the detriment of the second—or vice versa—does not respect the data furnished by the Gospel writings either. To distinguish between a conservative Christianity that recognizes the salvific value of the earthly Jesus, his teaching, and his pre-Easter activity and a progressive-Pauline Christianity whose salvific value proceeds exclusively from the cross and the resurrection does violence to the historical reality of the primitive Church.

There is continuity, then, between the kerygma and the pre-Easter Jesus, between the faith of the community and the historical event. The faith of the Church does not constitute a wall that separates us irremediably from the historical Jesus. "The Church did not 'invent' the kerygma. It only prolonged the message of Jesus and made it explicit. . . . The Easter faith is nothing other than a correct understanding of the historical Jesus. The kerygma of the Church was the only true interpretation it was possible to give to the fact of Jesus."[6]

To isolate the Christ recognized and announced by the Christian faith from the historical Jesus is just as arbitrary as the effort to attain the Jesus of history outside the faith of the Church, i.e., outside the understanding of Christ expressed in the New Testament writings.

The importance of the historical Jesus for the Christian faith, the indissoluble bond and the continuity that exist between him and the Christ believed and proclaimed in the Church, thus come to light.

The new investigation into the historical Jesus initiated after the Second World War has thus changed perspective with respect to the *Leben-Jesu-Forschung* of the last century. The question can no longer be posed according to the criteria and the purpose of nineteenth century positivism: to obtain the objective facts, the exact chronological succession of the events, in short, to reconstruct a history of Jesus in a biographical, chronicling, or psychological sense. The available documents—the Gospels—do not allow us to reach the historical Jesus in a pure state, abstracting from the faith of the primitive Church and the theological view of the evangelist. Consequently, the relation between kerygma and Jesus of Nazareth, between faith and history, is also changed: they are inseparable realities. Knowing the *bruta facta* is of no help to faith. One must understand them and understand them according to the interpretation of faith given in the kerygma. For many witnesses of his passion, Jesus was just one condemned man among so many others, and his death, even if followed in the particulars, did not have a special value. Understanding in faith is necessary in order to grasp in this slaying the salvific importance it has "for me" and to understand that it regards me personally because it is a death "for our sins."

It is therefore not sufficient to know the facts in their material nature, the exact unfolding of an event: it is necessary to grasp them in their revelational and salvational value. It is thus quite natural that the primitive Church in referring to the earthly life of Jesus was never directly interested in the *bruta facta* and does not describe them.

The very nature of the apostolic preaching invites us to pose correctly the question of the historical Jesus and his tie with the Christian faith: for the latter, it is not important to know the exact unfolding of an event, nor even to be able to prove that such a thing took place materially, but it is important that—whether demonstrable or not—the event be rooted in the experience of Christ, that it reflect a lived reality, that it be in harmony with his being and his message. It is not a question of knowing Jesus by means of an exact report on his existence and activity but of understanding him, of encountering him in his deep reality unveiled in faith, in the authentic meaning of his salvific action and of the mystery of his person: this is the necessary "historical" continuity between Jesus of Nazareth and the Lord believed and announced in the kerygma. There is no need to demonstrate the authenticity of every utterance of Jesus or the historicity of every account in order that the Christian faith be true.[7]

Fr. Mussner writes: "In reality, with regard to the historical Jesus, it is not first of all a question of knowing if the faith in Jesus is historically 'secured,' but if in the message one has spoken in a correct way about Jesus of Nazareth."[8] And W. Kasper writes: "History cannot serve the legitimation of the kerygma. But history does serve as a criterion of the kerygma and of faith."[9]

The result of the *Leben-Jesu-Forschung* was felt in this period as a failure because it sought to attain beyond the apostolic kerygma an impossible Jesus of Nazareth in the pure state. In reality, it was necessary to pose the question of the Gospel texts in a different way, not outside the faith that gave them birth. One thus realizes that their fidelity to the Jesus of history is immensely great, even if not according to the criteria of positivist research. M.-J. Lagrange was perfectly right already in 1928 when he wrote in the preface of his book *L'Evangile de Jésus-Christ:* "The Gospels are the only life of Jesus that can possibly be written."

It seemed necessary to me to make this preamble before broaching the topic true and proper. It is in fact important to be able to situate oneself well with regard to the Gospel text in order to be able to interrogate it from the proper perspective.

The Gospel writings mirror the originality of the Christian faith, the relation between the apostolic preaching and the historical Jesus. They are inseparably *confession of faith* of the community and *memory* of Jesus of Nazareth, Christian interpretation and faithful witness to what Jesus said and did.

It follows, on the one hand, that the nature of the text is such that it is no longer possible to know the facts of the life of Jesus—those related in the Gospel—in their precise unfolding according to the demands of a positivist view of history: this is the result at which research on the historical Jesus in the nineteenth century unwillingly arrived. On the other hand, the same nature of the Gospel text tells us that we can welcome its testimony with full trust and see in it the interpretation and thus the authentic understanding of the Jesus event, even if we are not in a position to verify the facts scientifically. Faith, it is true, does not stand directly on the fact but on its salvific interpretation.

The pessimism that followed on the failure of the *Leben-Jesu-Forschung* is not justified either. The originality of the Christian faith, and consequently of the Gospel text, consists in always being—by its nature—anchored in history, in an historical person: it is a testimony that rests on the real.

Consequently, we can concentrate our attention with trust on what truly interests the evangelist: the *theological dimension* of the narrated event.

Notes

1. Complete bibliographical information on the books and articles cited in the course of this work can be found at the end of this volume.

2. Bultmann, however, is not uninterested in the historical Jesus, since in 1926 he wrote his *Jesus,* an existential interpretation of the teaching of Christ. In the introduction, the author specifies: "In the following exposition, I have not considered this question (of the personality and life of Jesus) at all, not ultimately because one knows nothing certain about it, but because I consider it a secondary question." Bultmann's interest is directed to the "work" of Jesus insofar as a person's work is the reason he engages himself and takes a position. The work expresses what Jesus willed and thus is an expression of the understanding of his being-in-the-world.

The work of Jesus is identified with his teaching, understood not as a doctrinal system of truth but as Jesus' way of understanding himself and his own existence in history. In this case, the teaching of Jesus is understood as an interpellation directed to the reader or to the believer, an interpellation that regards my personal understanding in history and illuminates my choice.

Yet, it is not Jesus in himself that interests Bultmann but the teaching contained in the Gospels. He writes: "Tradition names Jesus as the bearer of these thoughts; in all probability, he actually was. But even if things were different, it would not change what is said in this tradition at all" (*Jesus,* [Munich: Siebensten Taschenbuch Verlag, 1967], 14).

3. Published in 1921. Together with a publication of M. Dibelius (1919) and of K. L. Schmidt (1919), it stands at the origin of the so-called *Formgeschichte* which studies the formation and the history—at the oral stage—of the literary units contained in the Gospels.

4. E. Käsemann, "Das Problem des historischen Jesus," in *Exegetische Versuche und Besinnungen,* 4th ed. (Göttingen: Vandenhoeck und Ruprecht, 1965), I:196.

5. Bultmann's disciples remain faithful, however, to the existentialist interpretation of the texts. Only the problem of the Christ announced in the kerygma is shifted to the Jesus of history.

It is the understanding Jesus had of himself, of his existence, and his call to decision that interpellate me today, when one must recognize the call of God and not only the Christ of the kerygma.

The divinity of Christ, his being as Son, and his resurrection remain for these exegetes an objectification that Christian faith has made, beginning from a purely internal reality that does not correspond to any external reality. Thus, the divine sonship of Christ says that God reveals in him the type of salvific relationship that he has established with me; the resurrection is the meaning that faith gives to the death of the Crucified.

On what, then, does the value of the historical Jesus rest? One has to ask if the experience of the historical Jesus does not risk becoming a myth also.

6. G. Minette de Tillesse, *Le secret messianique dans l'Evangile de Marc,* Lectio divina 47 (Paris: Cerf, 1968), 461.

Let us not forget, however, that even though he was, theologically speaking, constitutive for faith—i.e., even though his person and earthly activity already have a salvific value—insofar as he is the Son sent by the Father and insofar as his presence in the world inaugurates the eschatological times, the earthly Jesus does not constitute the whole of revelation.

The resurrection confirms and illuminates his previous existence, his authority, and his unique relationship to God, but it also bears something new. The kerygma cannot be reduced to the understanding of the earthly life of Jesus in the light of Easter; there is also newness in the resurrection itself.

7. Written in the light of the post-Easter faith and in view of the present situation of the community, the Gospels are not so much interested in who Jesus *was.* Rather, they wish to put believers in contact with the Jesus who is currently alive and present. To the basic fidelity to the historical datum—the past serves to illuminate Christ currently present and to give a countenance to his lordship—there also correspond a creativity and a freedom typical of the Easter faith in transmitting the tradition about Jesus and of Jesus, but always in the service of the salvific meaning of the work of Christ and of the profound mystery of his person.

This freedom goes so far as to place on the lips of Jesus words that he never uttered historically. In doing so, the Church did not have the slightest feeling of "inventing" something or, even worse, of falsifying the data. By creating "utterances of Jesus," the apostolic Church remained perfectly faithful to Christ himself: it had no one else on whom to stand! Of course, it is not a formal, bureaucratic fidelity. Convinced of expressing the authentic faith, certain of having the Spirit of Christ, it acted in the certainty that its very teaching must be transmitted as the teaching of Jesus, at least in certain cases.

"With H. Braun, J. Robinson, and others, one must therefore correctly distinguish between 'material authenticity' and 'authenticity with respect to Jesus' (*'Ipsissima Jesu'*). What the Christian communities say, or what their charismatic prophets say to the community in the name of the glorious Christ, may in fact reflect a basic attitude of the earthly Jesus and thus be 'authentic with respect to the content,' whereas the earthly Jesus may never have mentioned it" (E. Schillebeeckx, *Gesú, la storia di un Vivente* [Brescia: Queriniana, 1976], 81).

8. "Der 'historische' Jesus," in *Presentia salutis* (Düsseldorf: Patmos, 1967), p. 80, n. 30.

9. *Jesus der Christus* (Mainz, 1974), 39.

CHAPTER 1

The Account of the Death of Jesus (Mk 15:33–39) and Interpretation of the Text

If we now consider the account of the passion—and more particularly of the death of Jesus—it then becomes clear that we cannot read it like a simple chronicle. Even if it is based on incontestable historical facts,[1] it is still not the intention of the evangelist to give a report of the trial of an innocent man unjustly condemned to crucifixion. Mark's aim is not a strictly historical one, even if the evangelist remains substantially faithful to history. He is not worried about the chronology and the detailed exposition of the events in their exact succession. His purpose is to lead the reader to discover the meaning of the event. He is not interested in the *how* but in the *why*.

His account obviously belongs to history and not to legend. Nevertheless, the reader cannot fix his attention on the historical information. He should concentrate on the mystery, on the scandal of the cross, in which salvation is realized. Through the *deeds* that have taken place, the believer is led to discover what God *has done* for man.

"Just as Mark does not look for emotional effects, he does nothing to satisfy curiosity. He places the Christian community before the disconcerting event in all its crudeness and obliges it to examine itself and to take a stand," as A. Pronzato writes.[2]

A consideration of a general nature confirms what has been said thus far. In antiquity no author would have liked to dwell on such an infamous death as the crucifixion, even if it was widespread. Now, the passion of Christ turns out to be the most exhaustive account of this kind of execution in all of ancient literature.[3] And if the evangelists have dwelt on the crucifixion of Jesus, overcoming the discretion of their contemporaries concerning this cruel practice, it is certainly not due to a morbid curiosity of theirs but because that death had a profound meaning for their faith. We should therefore not expect a simple narration of the events.

The interpretation of the verses on the death of Jesus, which I should now like to make, will confirm this. These verses provide the context into which the cry of abandonment is inserted.[4]

The Text

Mk 15:33: "When noon came darkness fell on the whole earth and lasted until mid-afternoon.

34: At that time Jesus cried in a loud voice, *'Eloi, Eloi, lama sabachthani?'* which means, 'My God, my God, why have you abandoned me?'

35: A few of the bystanders who heard it remarked, 'Listen! He is calling on Elijah!'

36: Someone ran off, and soaking a sponge in sour wine, stuck it on a reed to try to make him drink. The man said, 'Now let's see whether Elijah comes to take him down.'

37: Then Jesus, uttering a loud cry, breathed his last.

38: At that moment the curtain in the sanctuary was torn in two from top to bottom.

39: The centurion who stood guard over him, on seeing the manner of his death, declared, 'Clearly this man was the Son of God!' "[5]

Mk 15:33: "When noon came, darkness fell on the whole earth and lasted until mid-afternoon."

It is certainly difficult to render this phenomenon historically credible—even if it is considered as a miracle—not only because the annals of the epoch do not relate such an extraordinary event for that date but also because darkness over the whole earth simply does not make sense from a meteorological point of view. One may then think that "the whole earth" is a biblical expression with which Palestine is often indicated. The darkness could then have come from an exceptional scirocco or a strong cloud formation over the land.

The reaction of the Hellenist Luke who attributes the phenomenon to an "eclipse of the sun" is interesting (Lk 23:44). He is seeking a rational explanation in natural causes for an event that he also considers as miraculous. But let us not treat this evangelist like a simpleton: he probably knew that at Easter—i.e., at the time of the full moon—an eclipse of the sun is impossible and besides never lasts three hours. Like the other Synoptic writers, Luke sees there a supernatural phenomenon, but by adding "with an eclipse of the sun" he shows that a miracle does not go against nature.[6]

After having found the problem insoluble on the level of history, some have referred to the usage in antiquity of making similar phenomena intervene at the death of famous personages like Romulus and Caesar. These phenomena are legendary features that show how nature participates in such a death as a sign of mourning. Even in Jewish literature extraordinary phenomena are related as having taken place at the death of certain rabbis.[7]

This rhetorical device, however, does not explain our passage for the simple reason that the darkness *precedes* the death of Jesus.

In reality, Mark 15:33 should be read neither as a legend nor in an historical perspective.

"It is not necessary to see an astronomical phenomenon (e.g., an eclipse of the sun) or a meteorological one (a cloud formation) in the darkness that accompanies the death of Jesus. It is rather an element of the literary and theological work intended to concretize the sense of the death of Jesus."[8]

The Fourth Gospel does not know this event, and in the Synoptics themselves apparently nothing happens during the three hours of darkness. Those present at the time do not react but behave "as if nothing were the matter." The account thus appears "empty."

We certainly find ourselves before a text that has been inserted for its theological, not its historical value; it is intended to shed light on the meaning of the death of Jesus. But since the evangelists do not render explicit the sense they attribute to this darkness, exegetical efforts are reduced to hypotheses.

In the Old Testament, darkness is part of a cliché used to announce the "Day of Yahweh," i.e., the day of the great judgment at the end of time. One thinks in particular of Amos 8:9: "On that day, says the Lord God, I will make the sun set at midday and cover the earth with darkness in broad daylight."

Mark 15:33 thus belongs to the prophetic and apocalyptic language and wishes to express the *universal* and *eschatological* meaning of the death of Christ which inaugurates the judgment of the world.

Other exegetes refer to the second-last plague of Egypt in Exodus 10:22: "So Moses stretched out his hand toward the sky, and there was dense darkness throughout the land of Egypt for three days." In this case, the darkness which precedes the death of Jesus would present the latter as the new "exodus," i.e., the passage to glory through the death of the cross.

More subtle, finally, is the hypothesis that insists on the fact that the darkness of which the evangelist speaks ceases before the death of Jesus. The death of Christ thus means precisely the end of darkness; it marks a turning point for the history of the world; it is a new beginning.

Whatever the case may be, let us bear in mind that Mark 15:33 is not the news report of an historical event but perhaps an apocalyptic cliché to suggest the cosmic and eschatological dimensions of what is happening on the cross.

This verse is followed by the cry of Jesus:

Mk 15:34:"At that time Jesus cried in a loud voice, 'Eloi, Eloi, lama sabachthani?' "

The mention of the ninth hour appears to repeat the indication of the preceding verse, but its origin is different, as we shall soon see. In all probability, it provides us with a reminder of the hour of Jesus' death.

At that hour, according to the accounts of Mark and Matthew, Jesus utters the last words pronounced on the cross: the beginning of Psalm 22.

Mark transmits the word in Aramaic, the language spoken in Palestine. In Matthew, on the other hand, the interpellation "My God, my God" (Eli, Eli) is Hebraized, whereas the question remains in Aramaic.[9] The change from "Eloi" (Mk) to "Eli" (Mt) is to be attributed to Matthew who seeks to assimilate "Eli" to "Elia" phonetically in order to render the misunderstanding between the name of God "Eli" and that of the prophet "Elia" more plausible.[10]

The cry of Jesus does in fact provoke a reaction among those present:

> *Mk 15:35–36:* "A few of the bystanders who heard it remarked, 'Listen! He is calling on Elijah!' Someone ran off, and soaking a sponge in sour wine, stuck it on a reed to try to make him drink. The man said, 'Now let's see whether Elijah comes to take him down.' "

These verses raise numerous questions with which the following chapter will deal in part. In popular Jewish belief, the prophet Elijah was invoked as the helper of the people or of the just man in the case of dire need.

Who are those present? The Roman soldiers standing guard? Bypassers, including the high priests and the scribes (cf. vv. 29, 31)? One may think that the person who offers the sponge soaked in vinegar to Jesus is a soldier; but then his remark (v. 36), which presupposes a good knowledge of the Jewish belief he shares, is not explained. That is scarcely probable for a Roman, not even for a soldier of the neighboring Syria who understood the Aramaic language. In fact, Matthew seems to want to clarify the ambiguity, since the sentences "Leave him alone. Let's see whether Elijah comes to his rescue" are uttered by those present. If it is a question of the Jews, particularly of the high priests and scribes, how does one explain the misunderstanding between the name of God and Elijah, between Eloi/Elohi (or better: Elahi) and Elijjahu?

Above all, how is it possible that they did not realize that Jesus was saying the beginning of Psalm 22 which they knew very well?

How is one to understand the offer of vinegar? In John (19:28–29), it appears as a gesture of compassion following on the words of Jesus: "I am thirsty." In John and in Mark/Matthew the allusion to Psalm 69:22 which comes from the tradition rather suggests an opposite meaning:

> " . . . they put gall in my food,
> and in my thirst they gave me vinegar to drink."

The Romans had the custom of offering this refreshing drink to the one crucified in order to reanimate him and thus to augment his sufferings. In the present context of the Gospel of Mark, the gesture acquires a further meaning: it prolongs Jesus' life in order to see if Elijah will intervene, or, better, to show precisely that the prophet does not help him and thus that Jesus dies abandoned by all heavenly help.

Thus, these two verses evidently present tensions on the literary level, superimpositions of meanings, which denote an evolution in the course of the transmission and an imperfect fusion of diverse traditions.

But before the unknown person can carry out his intention:

Mk 15:37: " . . . Jesus, uttering a loud cry, breathed his last."

Mark uses the same expression—"a loud cry"—which introduces the cry "My God . . . " of v. 34.

Is it a question of the same cry or of a second, inarticulate cry? The evangelist does not specify.[11] Matthew, on the other hand, clearly distinguishes it from the first cry by adding "once again" (Mt 27:50).

We probably stand before a precise historical recollection: the surprising cry of a crucified person who normally dies slowly of exhaustion from asphyxia and loss of blood.

Note the extreme sobriety of the evangelist; there is no outburst of sentimentalism, no pathos.

The account continues with two "signs":

Mk 15:38: "At that moment the curtain in the sanctuary was torn in two from top to bottom."

From an historical point of view, the question arises: Which curtain is at issue?

If there is an allusion to the curtain situated before the holy of holies, the innermost part of the temple where only the high priest could enter once a year, it is possible to see in this sign the fact that in the death of Jesus access to God became free for all men, Jews and pagans; or again, that in the crucified Jesus the curtain has fallen that prevented one until then "from seeing God in the splendor of his weakness."[12]

If the indication concerns the external curtain which closed the entrance of the temple and was visible to all, one could see there a reference to the future destruction of the temple "made by human hands" and, more generally, to the surpassing of the Jewish cult. Faith in the crucified and risen Jesus opens man to a new relationship with God, one no longer bound to the cult of the temple and to the old covenant, which has thus lost its function as the place of the presence of Yahweh. This rather polemical meaning could find confirmation in the words of Jesus with regard to the temple (Mk 13:2; 14:58).

In reality, the posing of the question in an historicizing perspective, i.e., the question whether the internal or the external curtain is at issue, is again a false problem: "Here also, as with the phenomenon of darkness (Mk 15:33 par.), it is not so much a question of fixing a historical fact as rather of giving a theological explanation of the death of Jesus."[13]

As in v. 33, we stand before a "visual theology."

It is necessary, then, to take the image of the torn curtain in its totality, as P. Lamarche suggests, and to see there a negative and a positive aspect: "A curtain that is torn from top to bottom is at the same time an irremediable destruction and a decisive opening."[14]

To see in the torn curtain—in relation to the death of Christ—both the end of the Jewish cult and the beginning of a new mode of God's presence is to see two meanings that are not mutually exclusive.

But, as P. Lamarche gives us to understand, one's attention should be directed to Jesus on the cross; the sign of the torn curtain unveils something of the mystery of the dying Christ.

"In Mark . . . the image of the curtain is given in a brutal way, without explanation, without accompaniment; it is tightly inserted into a scene that takes place entirely on Calvary. Everything happens as if the imagination of the reader were not to leave Christ on the cross for a single instant. The curtain that is torn should appear as if it were superimposed on the cross. There is a sort of identification between Christ and the temple in such a way that his death is felt, visualized, and understood as a laceration, with all the profound and diverse meaning that this image can bear when it is a question of the divine sanctuary" (p. 126).

Jesus on the cross, totally emptied and opened, has become the new temple not made by human hands. The reality of the resurrection is tied, discreetly but certainly, to the image of the torn curtain as applied to the crucified Jesus.

This meaning comes very close to the one expressed in Hebrews 10:20: we have access to intimacy with God "by the new and living path he has opened up for us through *the veil* (the 'veil' meaning *his flesh*)." The author of the epistle identifies the body of the crucified Jesus with the curtain: the crucified Jesus who dies "with a loud cry" thus becomes the tear in the vault of heaven, the "opening" that puts God and man into contact with one another.[15]

The evangelist has a second sign follow on that of the torn curtain: the centurion's confession of faith:

Mk 15:39: "The centurion who stood guard over him, seeing the manner of his death, declared, 'Clearly this man was the Son of God!'"

Let us note with what insistence Mark joins this verse to v. 37: the centurion stands *in front of* the Crucified and *sees* how he dies. For Mark, this confession of faith before the Crucified has a particular value. His whole Gospel is oriented toward it: the deep reality of Christ can be understood only in the light of his death. Jesus can be believed in authentically as the Son of God only by "looking at" the Crucified.

There is no need to lose oneself in questions of an historicizing nature on account of this verse either: How can this pagan bear witness to the Christian faith even before the resurrection of Jesus, before the apostles, simply because he sees a condemned man expire on the cross?

One could be tempted to see in this scene a legendary trait common to the "martyr accounts," a genre known in Judaism: the executioner is overwhelmed by his victim who dies bearing witness to the true religion.[16] It is very probable that this confession of faith was indeed inserted into a "theology of martyrdom" and therefore already existed in the tradition taken up by Mark. The expression "Son of God" without an article, which seems to refer to Wisdom 2:18, would confirm this. It indicates the One who has been chosen by God. We will speak of it again in Chapter 4.

There is no doubt, however, that in the text of Mark the proclamation of the centurion goes beyond this fact, for we are in the presence of a true confession of Christian faith before the crucified Jesus. The declaration of the centurion is attenuated in the other Synoptic Gospels. Luke seems to underscore the innocence of Jesus recognized by the soldier: "Surely this was an innocent man!" (Lk 23:47). Matthew, who preserves the title "Son of God," does not however present the proclamation as a confession of faith but as an expression of fear: the centurion, in fact, is struck not by the death of Jesus but by the earthquake (cf. Mt 27:54). In Mark, on the other hand, as I have already said, the proclamation constitutes the Gospel's point of arrival. In reality, this man represents all those who believe in Christ, and in a particular way the pagans. Before the Crucified, and through the mouth of the centurion, the Christian community expresses its faith in the crucified Jesus, the Son of God (cf. Mk 1:1).

The interpretation of the passage on the death of Jesus according to the Gospel of Mark permits us to understand better the immediate context in which the sole utterance is placed which, both in this Gospel and in Matthew's, Jesus "cried in a loud voice" from the cross. The analysis of the text has only confirmed what came to light in the introduction: the passion of Jesus is not to be read as a mere report of the events, nor as an account that opens onto the marvelous or the mythical, but as an account of the facts—above all, of one incontestable and fundamental fact, the death on the cross, which opens itself to the reflection of the Christian faith.

In particular, in the passage we have examined, one cannot deny the central position the death of Jesus occupies; all that precedes and follows converges on it. The death itself is set against the background of "signs"—the darkness, the torn curtain, the centurion's confession of faith—which serve to interpret it after the manner of a "visual theology."

Within this context, then, we find the cry of abandonment, Psalm 22:2, uttered by Jesus.

In such a context, one obviously cannot consider this articulated cry as a simple chronicle detail. It will certainly have, in harmony with all that surrounds it, a theological value in relation to the death of Jesus.

We shall see this better later on. Now it is necessary to face the historical problem: Did the crucified Jesus, historically speaking, cry out the beginning of Psalm 22:2 before expiring?

Notes

1. Cf. D. Dormeyer, *Der Sinn des Leidens Jesu*, Stuttgarter Bibel-Studien, no. 96 (Stuttgart, 1979), 28ff.

2. *La passione di Cristo. Un cristiano comincia a leggere il vangelo de Marco* (Torino: Gribaudi, 1980), III:6–7.

3. Cf. M. Hengel, *La crucifixion*, Lectio divina, no. 105 (Paris: Cerf, 1981), 39.

4. I shall choose the text of Mark and in doing so follow the opinion accepted by almost all exegetes, namely, that the Gospel of Mark was chronologically the first to be written.

It has also served as a source for Matthew, the other evangelist who relates the cry of abandonment (Mt 27:46).

A complete study would demand examining Matthew's point of view as well. A work of this kind has been done by B. Gerhardsson, "Jésus livré et abandonné d'après la Passion selon saint Matthieu," *Revue biblique* (April 1969):206ff. I shall summarize his study.

Matthew presents Jesus as the one who knows the Scriptures perfectly and does them, i.e., he lives the word of God. "In a general way, it is important to note that Matthew presents Jesus as a man instructed in the Scriptures, with the word of God in his heart and on his lips" (p. 211).

For the evangelist, it is therefore clear that Jesus is never caught unawares by the events, not even by his death on the cross. He knows the *hour* foreseen by God, the hour of the trial, in which God delivers him to his enemies. When the hour has come, Jesus delivers himself to his adversaries so that they can torture him and kill him. Christ's decision to deliver himself freely corresponds to the "Yes" said from the depths of his heart to that which God commands, "an intimate decision to accept the decree of God which is realized in the painful course of the events. The Son does not only obey in words and deeds but also 'in his heart' " (p. 217).

Jesus' silence during the passion only underscores this submission to the Father: "I was speechless and opened not my mouth, because it was your doing" (Ps 39:10) (cf. p. 218).

When, therefore, Jesus utters the cry of abandonment in the words of Scripture (Ps 22), he shows that he is living them not only in words and deeds but also in his heart: he is totally present to himself in that cry. "The key to the entire section (of the crucifixion) is the single utterance of Jesus noted there, Jesus' cry of 'abandonment.' . . . The 'curse' that strikes Jesus is the trial that will crown his submission and his love for God. Now he will reveal whether he loves his God and Father 'with all his heart, with all his soul, and with all his strength (mamon)' " (pp. 212–220).

"For Matthew it is most clear that Jesus on the cross experiences his situation as a total abandonment by God, as the 'hour' in which the horrors of the 'curse' pile up before him, in which the nearness of the God of blessing gives him neither consolation nor help, and in which exclusion by the human community runs parallel to abandonment by God.

Matthew, however, does not seem to suppose that Jesus lost his understanding of the 'will of God' for even an instant. It is clear that he sees
Jesus die enlightened by understanding, by faith, by hope (. . .), 'remember' what God has said and done, and then 'hope' for future salvation
and re-entrance into communion with his God when the time of 'deliverance' and 'abandonment' has passed.

"It is certainly not by chance that Jesus on the cross 'remembers,' re-
cites from memory . . . a word of Scripture that fits perfectly. That very
clearly fits into the whole of the account: Jesus has the 'word of God'
inscribed in his heart or, in a more prosaic manner, he has a living knowledge of Scripture. He thus finds in himself the teaching and the rule of
conduct that help him to advance even through darkness and abandonment (cf. Ps 119:105). The word of God inscribed in his heart cannot be
wrested from him. . . .

"The abandonment of Jesus considered as a trial is a classical theme.
One finds this theme, for example, in a condensed form in what is said
about Hezekiah: 'God forsook him to test him, that he might know all
that was in his heart' (2 Chr 32:31)" (pp. 224–225).

In the conclusion, Gerhardsson presents the cry of abandonment in
the total picture of the Gospel:

"What Jesus did from his baptism to the tomb was determined by the
will of God and can be divided into *two periods*. In the first period, he
is under the 'blessing,' he operates 'with power,' God is 'with him.' In
the second period, he is under the 'curse,' he acts in 'weakness,' God has
'delivered and abandoned' him. The trial has reached its summit. But
both when God is with him and when God abandons him, he shows the
'perfection' of which the law and the prophets speak and which can be
summarized in the commandment: 'You shall love the Lord your God
with your whole heart, with your whole soul, and with all your mind';
this includes the other: 'You shall love your neighbor as yourself'
(22:34–40; cf. par.). In the activity of Jesus, Matthew sees 'the perfectly
just one' who incarnates the attitude of love . . . and can therefore serve
as a model for both the strong and the weak, since Jesus has shared the
condition of both" (pp. 226–227).

5. The Italian original follows the New Testament translation of An-
gelico Poppi, *Sinossi dei quattro Vangeli*, ed. Messaggero (Padova,
1972). The English translation will use the New American Bible translation unless otherwise noted. The word "abandoned" will be consist-
ently used for "forsaken." In this citation, "countryside" in v. 33 has
been changed to "earth."

6. Cf. A. Georges, *Etudes sur l'oeuvre de Luc,* Sources bibliques (Paris: Gabalda, 1978), 144.

7. For example: "When Rabbi Acha expired, the stars became visible at noon," in Strack and Billerbeck, *Kommentar zum Neuen Testament aus Talmud und Midrasch* (Munich, 1926), I:1040.

8. Ingo Hermann, *Evangelium nach Markus* (Düsseldorf, 1965), II:144. I shall at once mention the suggestive but not totally convincing hypothesis of Fr. W. Danker, "The Demonic Secret in Mark: A Re-Examination of the Cry of Dereliction (15, 34)," *Zeitschrift für die neutestamentliche Wissenschaft* 1/2 (1970):48–69.

The author places the death of Jesus in the perspective of Mark who presents the ministry of Jesus as exposed to demonic hostility. This struggle against the forces of the devil reaches its summit in the cry of abandonment. Jesus appears as one possessed by the devil, completely engaged in an exorcism that costs him his life (cf. Mk 9:26): he expels the devil with a final cry (15:37) and expires. In this "demonological" dimension of the death of Jesus, the darkness (15:33) represents the most appropriate time for the demons and their operations.

9. According to J. Jeremias, even the Hebrew form of "Eli" comes from the Aramaic. "The cry on the cross in Mt 27:46 is to be attributed *in toto* to the words of Jesus handed on in Aramaic" (*Neutestamentliche Theologie. Die Verkündigung Jesu* [Gütersloher Verlagshaus, Gerd Mohn, 1971], 16).

The Aramaic word in its usual pronunciation was "Elahi." Mark's transcription—"Eloi" or "Elohi"—presupposes a dark "a." But there is no evidence for such a pronunciation in Palestine at the time of Jesus (cf. Th. Boman, "Das letzte Wort Jesu," *Studia Theologica* 17 [1963]:106).

10. A different opinion is held by M. Rehm, for example, in "Eli, Eli, lama sabachthani," *Biblische Zeitschrift* 2 (1958): 276, who considers the text of Matthew as the original. It then remains to be explained how "Eli" ever became the Aramaic "Eloi" (Elohi) in the tradition of Mark, thus rendering a phonetic proximity to "Elia" impossible (vv. 35ff.).

Rehm's explanation seems a bit too hasty to me: Mark changed the abnormal Hebrew form into the more common Aramaic lection.

11. The connection of this cry (v. 37) with the cry of abandonment (v. 34) is denied by J. Gnilka because this author gives an unconvincing apocalyptic interpretation to the last cry of Jesus. He therefore attributes a different sense to the cry of v. 37 from that of v. 34: not a cry of abandonment but one of victory or of judgment (*Das Evangelium nach Mar-*

kus, Evangelisch-katholischer Kommentar zum Neuen Testament [Zurich: Benziger/Neukirchener Verlag, 1979], II:323).

12. P. Lamarche, *Révélation de Dieu chez Marc,* Le point théologique, no. 20 (Paris: Beauchesne, 1976), 127. His study on the torn curtain (pp. 121–129) is very fine.

13. E. Lohse, *Die Geschichte des Leidens und Sterbens Jesu Christi,* (Gütersloh, 1964), 98.

14. Ibid., 126.

15. A close interpretation identifies the curtain with the celestial vault (according to an ancient cosmological representation). The death of Jesus lacerates this curtain which separates heaven from earth. Cf. Lamarche, 124.

16. Cf. Dormeyer, op. cit., 83.

CHAPTER 2

The Historical Problem

In Search of the Most Ancient Tradition

Before facing the historical question, it is necessary to examine the literary problem, i.e., to determine how old the tradition is that transmits Christ's cry of abandonment on the cross.

It will be expedient to begin by comparing among themselves the different accounts of the passion contained in the Gospels, and, more precisely, the words pronounced by Jesus on the cross.

Since Matthew depends directly on Mark, except for additions or variations of his own, the words of the Crucified in the Gospels of Luke and John remain to be considered.

Here is the synopsis:

Mk/Mt	Luke	John
My God, my God, why have you abandoned me?	23:34: Father, forgive them; they do not know what they are doing. 23:43: I assure you: this day you will be with me in paradise. 23:46: Father, into your hands I commend my spirit.	19:26f: Woman, there is your son. . . . There is your mother. 19:28: I am thirsty. 19:30: Now it is finished.

What this establishes is evident: the three accounts do not have any utterance of the crucified Jesus in common.

At a time in which concordism was in force, this fact did not create serious problems. The different utterances in the different

Gospels were added up, and one arrived at the conclusion that, historically speaking, Jesus made seven utterances on the cross. The cry of abandonment was fourth in chronological order. At the bottom of this historicizing reading was the conviction that the Gospels were direct recollections of the events, written straight off by witnesses such as the apostles (Mt and Jn), or disciples of the apostles (Mk and Lk).

The premise of this book has already given us to understand that such an approach to the Gospel text is no longer possible today.

It would be historically improbable that each evangelist would remember precisely those words of Jesus omitted by the others!

In reality, one must take into account the pre-history of the Gospels, their long period of formation beginning with either oral or written traditions. The evangelists worked on sources and documents arising in different Christian environments (kerygma, liturgy, catechesis, polemics against the Jews, etc.), not on direct recollections. Moreover, the evangelists are theologians, and in their work they also express their point of view, their understanding of Jesus, or respond to the demands of the community. Their intention is not to relate a chronicle of events.

It is precisely the divergences found between one Gospel and another which demonstrate that these authors did not wish to transmit an objective report of the death of Christ.

The Utterances of the Crucified in John and Luke

Let us look more closely at the accounts of John and Luke. Chronologically speaking, the Gospel of John was the last (canonical) Gospel to be written. It now seems certain that the author had available a passion source of his own and that he did not use the Synoptics directly.[1] There is then no doubt that the present text strongly mirrors both the style and the thought of the evangelist, who was not satisfied with transmitting his source but has reinterpreted it. Here is what R. Schnackenburg writes:[2]

The Johannine presentation of the passion of Jesus . . . shows unmistakably the peculiarity of Johannine theology. . . . No theologian had ventured before to let the glory of Jesus shine directly in the disgraceful trial against him, in his passion, and in his death. This paradoxical view was reserved for the fourth evangelist, who was stimulated and prepared for it through his theological mode of consideration, which places everything in the presence of his Christ. . . . Certainly, there are particular motifs that emerge in the Johannine presentation of the passion (. . .); but everything is ordered and subordinated to the primary concern of rendering the secret enthronement of Jesus on the cross, his exaltation there, and his hidden victory over the power of evil visible for the eyes of faith. The cross is the throne of Jesus (19:14–19), the exhalation of his life is the consummation of his work (19:30).

Schnackenburg characterizes the Johannine account of the passion of Christ very well: Jesus, in his royal dignity, master of himself and of the events, carries to completion the work the Father has entrusted to him. He appears majestic until death. He does not suffer the crucifixion but actively participates in this death which is his glorification. He thus realizes the declaration: "No one takes it (my life) from me; I lay it down freely" (Jn 10:18). In order to render this intention explicit, John removes, for example, the story of Simon of Cyrene so that Jesus himself carries his cross and thus shows himself master of his freely accepted destiny. The evangelist removes from the account everything that is humiliating or shameful, like the waves of derision of the various persons present and the cry of abandonment—if the latter ever was in his source.

It is certainly in this global perspective that one must understand the three utterances of the Crucified.

There is no doubt that in the utterance Jesus addresses to his mother and to the disciple he loved the theological element predominates over the historical datum, which is difficult to specify. Mary is presented as the new Zion or Eve, mother and figure of the Church; the disciple, in turn, represents the Church as the eschatological people of faith.

The symbolic, typological value that the figure of Jesus' mother acquires presupposes an already fully developed theological reflection.[3]

Even the other utterance, "I am thirsty," which has the greatest probability of dating back to the pre-Johannine tradition and of being historical, is nonetheless charged with theological meaning. "The source of living water for eternal life, from which all are invited to drink (Jn 4:10–13f; 7:37ff), is from sheer effusion itself parched with thirst," Urs von Balthasar explains.[4] It is, however, necessary to add that the evangelist does not dwell on this negative aspect. The connection with v. 30 suggests that Jesus was thirsting to pour forth the Spirit who is living water.

Finally, John has chosen the last utterance of Christ with particular care: "Now it is finished." The whole life of the incarnate Word was devoted to fulfilling the work for which he had been sent and which is carried to completion in the eschatological "hour." This "hour" has arrived. "Thus, the last utterance of Jesus interprets his suffering and dying as the crowning and culmination of the work that he has fulfilled in obedience."[5]

Each of these words is solidly rooted and prepared for in the Gospel itself. Let us recall the episode at Cana where Jesus, addressing his mother with the title of "woman," explicitly refers to his "hour." When the "hour" has come, Mary is present again and receives the title of "woman."

The theme of thirst and of living water—the gift of the Spirit—comes to light above all in chapters 4 and 7:37ff, whereas the theme of fulfillment runs through the entire Gospel. The last utterance of Christ is particularly connected with John 13:1 and thus presents the death of Jesus as the fulfillment of his love for those who are his.

The conclusion appears to be clear: the utterances of Jesus on the cross acquire their whole meaning in the light of the entire Gospel and especially in the light of the theological vision of John.

In such a context, the cry of abandonment "is not appropriate in the mouth of the Word of God who sits on the cross as on a throne of glory."[6] And, in fact, the evangelist does seem to want to exclude such an experience of solitude on the part of the Crucified when, precisely in view of the passion, he has Jesus say: "An hour is comming—has indeed already come—when you will be scattered and each will go his way, leaving me quite alone (yet I can never be alone; the Father is with me)" (Jn 16:32).

Luke also transmits three utterances of the crucified Jesus. The evangelist is familiar with the work of Mark and has used other traditions as well. Nevertheless, the redactional work remains important. Among other things, he constructs the account of the passion so as to present the behavior of Jesus as the perfect model for imitation:[7] Jesus, who is innocent, passes the great test of the passion in filial obedience and in total trust in the Father.

In this perspective, Jesus pardons his executioners, thereby being the first one to live his teaching on the love of one's enemies to the full (cf. Lk 6:27ff). "Father, forgive them; they do not know what they are doing" (Lk 23:34).[8]

The two brigands crucified next to Jesus themselves represent two types of attitude toward Jesus, the one negative, the other positive. The utterance of the good thief casts light on one aspect of Luke's soteriology: the fruit of the cross is conversion (see also Lk 23:48: the crowd "went home beating their breasts"). "The signs that accompany the death of Jesus are thus according to Luke not first of all cosmic-apocalyptic phenomena but a transformation taking place in the hearts of men."[9]

Jesus' response to the good thief is itself typical of Lucan thought (at least with respect to the other Synoptics): "I assure you: this day you will be with me in paradise" (Lk 23:43). By means of this word of Christ, Luke seems to want to correct a vision that expects salvation only at the end of time ("when you enter upon your reign," v. 42). Without denying the importance of the parousia of the Lord, the evangelist focuses attention on the *now* of this salvation and thus on the death of the individual (and not only on the collective eschatology in the perspective of the imminent coming of the kingdom of God).[10] Luke also expresses the reality of paradise not with apocalyptic images but in existential terms of relationship with Christ which recall the expressions of Paul and which in any case belong to a post-Easter language: "being with Christ" (cf. Phil 1:23; 1 Thess 4:17; also 1 Thess 5:10; 2 Thess 2:1; Rom 14:8).

Finally, the last utterance that Luke places on the lips of the dying Jesus comes from Psalm 31:6 (the evangelist adds the appellative "Father"). It was recited by the Jew as an evening prayer: "Father, into your hands I commend my spirit" (Lk 23:46). Thus, the evangelist expresses one last time the filial abandonment of Jesus into the hands of the Father.

If we take an overall view of the text of Luke, the sense of serenity and of peace which accompany Jesus predominates even in death. Obviously, it would be out of place to insert the cry of abandonment into such a context. Luke, who was familiar with this cry in the tradition of Mark, intentionally omits it and replaces it with the prayer from Psalm 31:6, as the introduction shows: "Jesus uttered a *loud cry*" (Lk 23:46). This cry is scarcely suitable to the content of the prayer of Psalm 31:6; it is an expression that comes from Mark 34:37.

Let us draw the conclusions from this doubtless very rapid investigation.

One fact, which is important for the correct understanding of the text, has become clear: the utterances of Jesus on the cross can be adequately interpreted only within the Gospel within which they are read, i.e., if one takes into consideration the theological thought proper to the evangelist who transmits them or writes them without mixing it with that of the others.

Adding up the utterances of the Crucified which are found in the different Gospels is an arbitrary operation that does not take account of the correct value and position these utterances acquire only in the context of their respective Gospel.

Consequently, it is necessary to respect the cry of abandonment in the Gospels of Mark and Matthew as the *only* articulate cry expressed by the crucified Jesus, "which only in the arbitrary cataloguing of a Gospel harmony can be relativized as the 'fourth utterance.' "[11] Only then will it be accorded the prominent position it requires in the account of the passion that probably already existed in the more archaic tradition.

We should make another observation: there exists a tendency

to attenuate the crudeness of the cry of abandonment. The apocryphal Gospel of Peter, written at the beginning of the second century, is particularly significant in this regard. It alters the text in the following way: "The Lord cried out, 'My strength, my strength, you have abandoned me!' " Jesus complains of feeling his physical energies diminish!

As we have seen, the Gospels of Luke and John simply omit the cry. Did they fear that it could be misunderstood by Christians of a Hellenistic culture? But to whom is Mark writing?

In any case, the tendency to present the death of Christ in a more dignified manner in the Gospels of Luke and John must have deeper motives: not the fear of the truth, nor even the influence of docetism. One must understand it as a demand of faith to penetrate beyond the crude reality to discover and illuminate the Mystery of unity which is at work there, the love which is at the bottom of all and constitutes the hidden glory of the incarnate Son. The experience of the presence of the Risen One in the community exerts an influence in this sense. There is, it is true, the risk of losing sight precisely of this "crudeness" to which the incarnation is joined and which is so essential to the faith.

But all this clearly speaks in favor of the antiquity of the tradition that relates the cry of abandonment.

The Pre-Marcan Tradition

Let us close our treatment of the utterances of the Crucified in the Gospels of Luke and John and return to the account of Mark, which represents the oldest account of the passion and death of Jesus accessible to us.

Is it possible to go beyond it? Can one retrace the history of the tradition that has given us the present text of Mark? Are we able to turn back the times and ascertain the age of the tradition that relates the cry of Jesus? Is it one of the most archaic elements, or was it introduced at a later period?

These questions presuppose that the account of the passion in Mark does indeed have a pre-history, that it is not simply an eyewitness report but that one must take into account the time factor—and thus the possibility of evolution—that separates the historical event from the present writing of Mark.

And, in fact, elements do exist in the account of Mark that show that it too was not written straight off but has a history of its own.

The interpretation of Mark 15:33–39 has furnished literary indications of this: the episode concerning Elijah and the vinegar offered to Jesus (vv. 35–36) has revealed several discontinuities and a significant superimposition of meanings. I should now like to draw attention to other elements that have not yet been taken into consideration.

The fact is quite surprising that in the account of Mark the entire crucifixion is inserted into a schema of three hours, a schema that the other evangelists no longer respect. Jesus is crucified at the third hour (i.e., at 9:00 A.M.: v. 25). The darkness covering the whole earth begins at the sixth hour (i.e., at noon) and is over at the ninth hour (thus, at 3:00 P.M.: v. 33).

It is unlikely that the evangelist is transmitting an historical datum here. It would be extremely fortuitous if the events had happened in intervals of exactly three hours. Luke tries to render the event more plausible by writing: "It was now around midday . . ." (Lk 23:44).

Above all, the hour of the crucifixion, the third hour, is in clear contradiction to what John writes: at the sixth hour (i.e., at noon) Jesus still found himself before Pilate (see Jn 19:14).

Two explanations predominate:

—We find ourselves before a liturgical schema. In fact, the hours mentioned do correspond to the traditional hours of Jewish prayer. Hence, the hypothesis: the account of the crucifixion was inserted into this liturgical schema when the community commemorated the passion of Christ, on Good Friday, for example.

—Others, however, see here an apocalyptic schema of the hours of the day: the events narrated in the third, sixth, and ninth hours are tending toward the twelfth hour, i.e., toward the end of the day, which had a symbolic value. The twelfth hour is the final hour *par excellence,* the hour that puts an end to the apoc-

alyptic events and introduces the judgment of God. This hour co-
incides precisely with the death of Jesus.

Whatever the case may be, the schema of the three hours appears as a superadded element that has "classified" the data of
the tradition on the crucifixion.[12]

The so-called "doublets" are another indication of literary
stitching. Mark refers twice to the crucifixion (vv. 24 and 25); he
twice mentions that Jesus cried out in a "loud voice" (vv. 34 and
37), etc. This fact suggests the confluence of two traditions.

These are a sample of some of the factors that lead exegetes to
research the history of the tradition of the account of the passion.

How then is the present narration constituted which we read
in Mark?

I cannot enter into the labyrinth of the various hypotheses. I
shall relate the principle ones only:

• The account is formed of small literary units that were originally isolated and then grouped together by some proto-Luke or
even by the evangelist himself. It is incontestable, as *Formgeschichte* has demonstrated, that even in the account of the passion
there exist more or less large literary units that have been placed
together. But one must also agree with R. Pesch when he affirms
that a great part of these literary units never existed indepen-
dently but were formed in view of a more ample account.[13] To
me it seems correct to believe that the Markan account of the passion is not the result of a literary puzzle.

• Some exegetes (J. Schreiber, for example) consider the present narration as the fruit of the more or less successful com-
bination of two originally independent traditions. This theory
rests in particular on the presence of doublets in the present
account.

• I should be inclined to think that at the beginning there existed a principal account that was amplified in time with other
elements like the apocalyptic ones without ultimately excluding
the hand of the evangelist himself. This first tradition in the Ar-

amaic language could date back to the community of Jerusalem.[14]

If then we get down to details, limiting ourselves to the already
examined episode of the death of Jesus (vv. 33–39), in order to
learn which of these verses belong to the primitive tradition and
which are later additions or come from Mark in person—if therefore we want to follow the literary tradition of Mark 15:34—
there is the risk of being disoriented and disappointed. In order
not to encumber our study, I shall relate the conclusions of several
recent works in a note.[15]

In spite of often contradictory results, a certain agreement exists in the recognition that v. 34a—the cry of abandonment—
dates back to the most ancient tradition. Reserve is practically
found only on the part of those who, following Bultmann, consider v. 34 as a later interpretation of the inarticulate cry of v. 37.

It is necessary to examine this affirmation more closely.

From the point of view of literary analysis, the opinion of Bultmann can be neither validated nor invalidated. Mark is imprecise,
and perhaps on purpose: the cry of v. 37 could very well be identified with that of v. 34. "The grammatical construction of v. 37
does not necessarily oblige one to think of a further, wordless cry
of Jesus. Rather, it is possible to relate 'uttering a loud cry' to the
cry mentioned in v. 34a."[16] Matthew, who read the same Markan
text, speaks instead of two distinct cries. We should therefore
limit ourselves to considerations of a more general nature.

A very widespread line of reasoning used to rebut the thesis of
Bultmann consists in affirming that the post-Easter community
would scarcely have placed such a cry on the lips of the dying
Jesus. It is unlikely that in order to render an inarticulate cry explicit Christians would have chosen precisely as the last words of
their Lord such a harsh utterance that could not have failed to
provoke difficulties for their own faith and to confirm the conviction of the Jews: one who is abandoned by God cannot be the
Messiah![17]

This argument is not very convincing to me. If in fact Psalm
22:2 could have been misunderstood in the Hellenistic commu-

nities, this is perhaps one of the reasons it was omitted by either Luke or John (but was Mark not also writing to a Hellenistic community?). It could not have been misunderstood in a Palestinian church, however, for the Jews knew Psalm 22 perfectly well, which is essentially a prayer of trust and praise. Even if Jesus cries out his loneliness—and the evangelist does place the accent on such an abandonment (as will be seen in the following)—the invocation is still directed to "my God," i.e., to Yahweh, to the God of the covenant with Israel, who is faithful from generation to generation. The appeal to "my God" therefore implies of itself trust in the God who has freely bound himself to his people and has said his "Yes" to man.[18] At least it was so in the mind of a Jew.

Indeed, it is neccessary to say even more: the primitive community seems not to want to hide this abandonment. In fact, even the understanding of the death of the son in the parable of the tenants was interpreted in this sense: "Then they seized and killed him and dragged him outside the vineyard" (Mk 12:8). This is an evident allusion to the death of Jesus. But the sentence fragment "and dragged him outside the vineyard" is not at all indispensable as a narrative element. Its presence is understood only by accepting the meaning contained there: Jesus dies outside the vineyard that is Israel, thus outside the covenant, outside the community of God, abandoned by the God of the law.

Finally, to affirm that the cry of the dying Jesus constitutes a difficulty for the community is to forget that the true difficulty, the scandal *par excellence,* is the *cross* itself. It is not only the wood of shame, the sign of social rejection; the "scandal of the cross" as experienced by the Jew has a religious character founded on Deuteronomy 12:23, as Hengel writes.[19] The cry of abandonment is included in what the cross of itself represented for a Jew. The cross implies abandonment; it is its sign.

Consequently, from the beginning—and especially at the beginning—the community not only did not have any difficulty in placing, if necessary, such a cry in the mouth of Jesus, but also had to do so because it had to look the cross in the face; it could not avoid it with the entire burden of its curse.

And that is a guarantee of the antiquity of the tradition that relates the cry of abandonment.

It is therefore necessary to remember how scandalous and contemptuous this pitiful end on the cross of one who claimed to be the Messiah must have appeared. According to the Jewish interpretation of Scripture itself (cf. Dt 21:23), death on a cross was the evident sign that the one upon it is not of God. The Christian community, born of the encounter with the Risen One, could not present its message in the Jewish world without resolving this scandal. It had to make others understand—and to understand first itself—that such a death is also in accordance with the Scriptures; it had to explain how it is possible that the one it recognized as the Anointed of God could come to an end on the wood of the curse.

The death of Jesus is a fact that challenges the faith itself of the Christian Church since it places the latter before the mystery of God who reveals himself in hiddenness, who manifests his salvific love in the failure and abandonment of the Just One. Following the Crucified requires a total reorientation.

A neutral and objective report of the passion and death of Jesus has therefore never existed. From the beginning, the episodes—for the most part of indubitable historical value—were chosen and formulated not with the aim of giving an exact description of what happened the 7th of April in the year 30 on Golgotha but with the intention of understanding this death according to the plan of God and of inserting it into the history of salvation. It must be read not as a newspaper item but as "narrative theology."

The theory of Bultmann according to which the tradition originally related only an inarticulate cry of the dying Jesus (cf. Mk 15:37a), a cry that only later received its interpretation with the help of Psalm 22, appears as a tempting construction of rational logic, but of a logic on paper that finds no counterpart in reality.

The study of the tradition of the passion leads in fact to the conclusion that, however closely one follows its history and its evolution, this tradition has already been constructed in the light of the Old Testament. In order to overcome the scandal of the cross, to understand with the eyes of faith all that happened on Calvary, the first community found particularly useful the Old Testament motif of the *passio justi* as well as the psalms of lamentation and the diptych of Wisdom 2:12–20; 5:1–7, which in Judaism translates the understanding of the suffering servant (Is 53). I shall return to this theme later.

For now, it is important to bear in mind that according to many exegetes the motif of the *passio justi* is present in the tradition of the passion from the very beginning.[20]

If the scenes of the crucifixion are taken into special consideration, one notes the great importance that Psalm 22, which belongs to the *passio justi* group, has had in the formation of this composition. References to this psalm are to be read in Mark 15:24 (= Ps 22:19); v. 29 (= Ps 22:8); and v. 34 (= Ps 22:2). Here we have a positive indication that allows us to think that v. 2 of this psalm (and thus the corresponding cry of Jesus in Mark 15:34) was present in the tradition from the beginning.[21]

H. Gese correctly concludes: "The oldest presentation of the central event of the death of Jesus is hidden under the veil of Psalm 22. With that we have before us not only an ancient interpretation of the death of Jesus but also, it seems to me, the most ancient understanding of the event on Golgotha."[22]

We have thus arrived at the end of the literary investigation. There exist, then, strong indications that allow one to think that the cry of abandonment of Jesus expressed with the help of Psalm 22:2 dates back to the origin of the tradition of the passion.

That, however, does not necessarily mean that it dates back to Jesus himself. It is now necessary to face the historical problem in order to learn whether the cry of abandonment was formulated by the very first community or whether it proceeds historically from the dying Jesus.

The Historical Problem

The community, then, has utilized Psalm 22 in the presentation of the account of the crucifixion. This fact, which permitted us to deduce the antiquity of the cry of abandonment in the tradition, now seems to turn against the historicity of this very cry since it leads to the logical conclusion that even v. 2 of the psalm which we read in Mark 15:34 is due to the elaboration of the community, just as the other passages are where the influence of this psalm is noticeable.

Other data seem to confirm the non-historicity of the cry of abandonment.

Th. Boman enunciates a first reason: the Gospels show that Jesus was not in the habit of expressing his thoughts with the help of citations from the Old Testament.[23]

But Boman's argument is weak: like every pious Jew, Jesus prayed with the psalms (cf. Mk 14:26) during his life and, like many, would have been able to die with the verses of a psalm on his lips.

The second reason of the author carries greater weight: "Jesus never exposed his inner life to the public and did so only seldomly to his disciples. He kept his personal relationship with God to himself. When he wished to speak with his heavenly Father in prayer, he sought out insofar as possible a lonely place. To his disciples also he recommended that they go into their chamber, close the door, and pray in secret. Should he then at the end of his life, and as its end, have confessed in prayer before the eyes of his enemies that God had abandoned him or, in any case, that he felt abandoned by God? Was he to have prayed this in a loud voice, not in a moment of psycho-physical weakness, but in full possession of this strength? Or did he perhaps gather his final strength to communicate this abandonment by God to posterity? If anyone ever gave what is holy to dogs or cast his pearls before swine, then it must have been on this occasion! There is no analogy for such a thing in the life of Jesus. A normal man would hardly have done so in such a situation, however disillusioned he may have died, unless, full of regret, he had intended to draw attention to his misspent life as a warning."

It is necessary, then, to take seriously into consideration the physical state of one condemned to the cross.

The preceding flagellation causes one to lose tremendous

amounts of blood, and thus the victim enters into a state of extreme weakness. Jesus experienced such weakness in a particular way, as the scene with Simon of Cyrene (cf. Mk 15:21) and Pilate's surprise at such a rapid death (cf. Mk 15:44) allow us to suppose.

Under these conditions, it is practically impossible that the Crucified would have had the strength to articulate an entire sentence in a loud voice. Moreover, one who has been crucified dies from slow asphyxiation, which renders every effort to speak extremely painful.

Ortensio da Spinetoli writes: "The specific cause by which crucifixion brings about death still remains mysterious." In a note, the exegete specifies: "The hypotheses are many: heart failure, syncope, muscular tetany, embolism, asphyxia, etc.; in such a case, death is accelerated by frequent hemorrhages, transudations of serum and plasma, together with thickening of the residual blood, which slowly blocks respiration and circulation. . . . According to La Cava, crucifixion modifies the position and the dimensions of the thoracic cavity and the respiration. Oxygenation becomes insufficient for nutrition of the tissues and then causes a progressive toxification."[24]

In spite of these data, the otherwise so surprising report that Jesus dies uttering "a loud cry" undoubtedly has historical value.

Another element at the center of the discussion on the historicity of the cry articulated by Jesus concerns the following scene, the misunderstanding about Elijah (Mk 15:35–36), which is certainly connected with the cry of Jesus.

But many things remain obscure. How are we to explain the confusion between Eloi and Elijah (or between Elahi and Elijjahu) on the part of those present, who are supposed to be Jews?

The temptation simply to consider the scene of the misunderstanding as secondary as a way of resolving the discrepancy is strong: Mark or his source would have added it subsequently without successfully hiding the tension between vv. 34 and 35.

But is it possible to judge the episode about Elijah as a creation of the community? Boman (p. 107) is right in reminding us that the Church has never invoked Elijah as a helper in times of trouble and would have supposed such an invocation for Jesus even less!

The episode must thus have a solid historical foundation. To affirm, as J. Gnilka does in his commentary, that the anecdote is primitive but that Mark alone would have put it in its present place is to conceal the fact that the misunderstanding of those present—"He is calling Elijah"—requires Jesus actually to have said something. The literary unity of vv. 35–36a could not have existed otherwise than in proximity to a cry of the crucified. Moreover, in the present plot, against the background of which the death of Jesus is placed, this scene appears almost as a disturbing factor in the Second Gospel. It is then difficult to make it date back to the redaction of Mark, who probably would have done without it.

Thus, one returns to the original problem: How are we to explain in such a case the confusion of names?

There have arisen different, more or less satisfying attempts at a solution:

• Jesus would have cited the psalm in Hebrew and thus would have said "Eli." But Eli is also the abbreviated name of the prophet Elijjahu. Those present therefore confused the name of God with the abbreviated name of the prophet (M. Rehm).

But this is a mere supposition. Analogous examples for the abbreviated name of Elijjahu are not known.

• Jesus would have said the entire verse of the psalm in Hebrew. The people who heard him, not knowing this language, were not able to understand the words of Jesus except for the term "Eli," which they then confused with the name of the prophet.

This is an ingenious hypothesis. But J. Gnilka, its author, does not take into account that, at least according to the data of Mark, some high priests and scribes were also present (Mk 15:31), who certainly understood Hebrew!

• Jesus would have cried, "Elijah." This form of the name of

God is in fact found once in the documents of Qumran. But its common usage is not assured.

One has the impression of moving in a field where there are no solutions. Nor is it necessary to concentrate the problematic only on the words "Eloi-Elijah." In reality, the crucified Jesus also uttered the continuation of the psalm ("lama sabachthani") and not only the term "Eloi." But this fact renders the explanation of the misunderstanding even more difficult.[25]

Seeing that there is practically no successful resolution of the misunderstanding, the possibility remains that it is a question of an infelicitous play on words. Thus M.-J. Lagrange in his commentary on the Gospel of Mark: "Ils font un méchant calembour et un calembour méchant." More recently, R. Pesch has also spoken of a deliberate and malicious distortion of meaning made by Jesus' enemies under the cross.

Even this solution, at bottom the only one possible for whoever recognizes the historicity of the cry and the following mockery of those present, leaves certain questions open. If in fact Jesus' adversaries had wanted to make fun of him, his cry would itself have been the best pretext for doing so, without having to invent an invocation of the prophet Elijah: he who claims to be the Messiah and the King of the Jews publicly confesses that he has been abandoned by God!

An ingenious explanation has been proposed by Th. Boman.[26] Accepting the historicity of the cry as certain, the author asks himself: What could Jesus have shouted that auricular witnesses would have understood as an invocation of Elijah?

Referring to Psalm 118:28 which he had sung together with his disciples a few hours before during the last supper, Jesus said: "Eli attâ," i.e., "My God, it is you."[27] He thus dies praising God: "Jesus coins a farewell word that on account of its brevity and contentual fullness was worthy of the great master: a cry of exultation to the Father, a greeting to the disciples, and a shout of triumph to the world" (p. 119).

But, Boman says, this exclamation was understood in different ways.

The Jews misunderstood: "Elijja tâ," i.e.: "Elijah, come!" The pronunciation is practically identical. The women, disciples of Jesus, who found themselves in the vicinity, heard on the contrary that this cry was directed to God. Subsequently, the disciples sought the text of the Old Testament to which Jesus was referring. The words "Eli attâ" are read four times, namely in Psalms 22:11, 63:2, 118:28 and 140:7.

John or his source found the expression "Eli attâ" in Psalm 63, where one reads: "For you . . . my soul thirsts," a verse which the evangelist condenses into the words of Jesus, "I am thirsty."

Luke read the corresponding expression in the Greek translation of Psalm 31, which also contains the sentence he then adapts to the situation of Jesus: "My days are in your hands."

Finally, Mark discovered the "Eli attâ" in Psalm 22:11 and therefore transcribed the beginning of this psalm: "My God, my God, why have you abandoned me?"

Unfortunately, the evolution of the Christian tradition in the earliest period does not follow the criteria of Boman. There was no guessing game. His hypothesis, which finds no support in the Gospel text, has been cautiously received by some[28] but is generally rejected with a smile: it is just too good to be true! R. Schnackenburg defines the attempt of Boman as "a pretty thesis."[29] One can only agree.

I have thus expounded a panoramic view of the questions and perplexities raised by the historical problem. Unfortunately, no Rosetta stone exists to help us exit from them. There are no decisive proofs either in favor of or against the historical authenticity of the crucified Jesus' cry of abandonment. R. Pesch affirms that the ancient tradition deserves greater trust in its historical value than it commonly enjoys.[30] According to this exegete, the pre-Markan account of the passion transmits the Aramaic prayer of the dying Jesus. And it is precisely Jesus' employment of the beginning of Psalm 22 that explains why the community made such great use of this psalm in the elaboration of the account of the passion (p. 495).

The result is not at all discouraging; rather, it confirms what I wrote in the introductory note.

The Gospel text itself invites us not to consider the utterance of Jesus as a simple chronicle item about the last instants of his life nor to stop at an historicizing reading, but to proceed to the essentials.

It is also necessary to overcome a psychological reading which risks enclosing the believer in a devotion to the crucified and abandoned Jesus without opening him to the newness of revelation that such a cry manifests. The evangelist and the tradition before him do not have the means in hand to sound the psychology of Christ, especially in such a unique and essential moment. The very sobriety of the text already invites us not to dwell on the psychological aspect. Moreover, the slight interest that Mark demonstrates in this aspect is seen in the fact that the two times in the account of the passion in which he seems to register feelings of Jesus—in the garden of Gethsemani and in the cry of abandonment—it is always a question of references to passages of the Old Testament: Psalm 42:6 and Psalm 22:2.

From this one obviously must not deduce that Jesus did not suffer with his whole being the loneliness and abandonment of which the verse of Psalm 22 speaks. A prolonged and excruciating torture such as that of the cross inevitably leads man to experience the most profound anguish. However, it is not on this suffering in its psychological aspect that the evangelist wishes to dwell but on the theological meaning of what is expressed in the cry.

The value and importance of the cry of Jesus for Christian faith are in fact theological: the incarnate Son of God lives obedience and thus love for the Father to the point of completely assuming the human condition of suffering, of loneliness, of anguish, and of distance from God, of which the cross—as wood of the curse—is the sign. In the final analysis, the cry of abandonment must be understood as a revelatory word of God on the death of Christ.

At this point the cry will be able to become for us a revelation of God himself and of his relationship with man as well as to be taken as a key to Christian behavior, as a demand to "carry the cross" (Mk 8:34).

Notes

1. In this pre-Johannine tradition, however, the Synoptic traditions have been mixed with other elements; thus Anton Dauer, _Die Passionsgeschichte im Johannesevangelium_ (Munich: Kösel-Verlag, 1972), 226.

2. _Das Evangelium nach Johannes,_ Herders theologischer Kommentar zum Neuen Testament IV, 3rd ed. (Freiburg-Basel-Vienna, 1979), III:246.

3. There are "tensions" between the word of Jesus (Jn 19:26) and v. 25 which introduces it: v. 25 mentions different women near the cross, whereas in v. 26 only Mary appears, and the others are ignored. On the other hand, v. 26 recognizes the presence of the disciple who is absent in v. 25. All this indicates a certain "stitching" at the literary level, the juxtaposition of material of different provenance. The mention of the presence of several women (v. 25) dates back no doubt to the source, whereas the following verse which contains the utterance of Jesus reflects the style and the construction of the evangelist. Thus, the title "woman" as an appellative addressed by Jesus to his mother is proper to John (cf. Jn 2:4). The existence of the disciple "whom Jesus loved" is also known only to him. A. Dauer, op. cit., 197, notes that even if John 19:26 has every appearance of coming from the evangelist, that does not mean that he invented the scene. That Jesus, before dying, entrusted his mother to the disciple seems very probable historically. It is possible that the evangelist took advantage of the mention by his source of the presence of women at the cross to place the scene at the foot of the cross and thus to elevate it to a more symbolic and theological dimension.

In fact, the supposition that this event took place at the foot of the cross runs up against certain difficulties:

The mention of the flight of the disciples (Mk 14:27–50), including Peter (cf. 14:29–31), a mention that John himself confirms (cf. Jn 16:32), contradicts the presence of the disciple whom Jesus loved at the foot of the cross.

If Jesus foresaw the nearness of his death, it is difficult to suppose that he waited until the very last minute to take care of his mother. Cf. A. Dauer, op. cit., 198–200.

4. "Mysterium paschale," in _Mysterium Salutis,_ ed. J. Feiner, M. Löhrer (Einsiedeln-Zurich-Cologne, 1969), III/2:213.

5. Dauer, op. cit., 210.

6. X. Léon-Dufour, _Face à la mort. Jésus et Paul_ (Paris: Ed. du Seuil, 1979), 159.

7. Cf. A. Vanhoye, "Structure et théologie des récits de la Passion dans les évangiles synoptiques," *Nouvelle Revue Théologique* 2 (1967):160–162.

8. There is some doubt about the authenticity of this utterance of Jesus. It is lacking in some of the important manuscripts such as the papyrus P75 from the beginning of the third century, the *Codex Vaticanus* of the fourth century, and in witnesses of different large manuscript families. For a discussion of this, cf. Georges, op. cit., 232. He holds this utterance to be authentic, since Luke presupposes it in Acts 7, 60.

9. H.-R. Weber, *Kreuz und Kultur,* Institut des sciences bibliques (Université de Lausanne, 1975), 106.

10. Cf. J. Dupont, *Les Béatitudes* (Paris: Gabalda, 1973), III:133–135.

11. Urs von Balthasar, "Mysterium paschale," op. cit., 212.

12. E. Linnemann, in *Studien zur Passionsgeschichte,* Forschungen zur Religion und Literatur des Alten und Neuen Testamentes, 102 (Göttingen, 1970), considers precisely these indications of the hours as the basic element of the primitive account. This thesis has not enjoyed a great consensus among the exegetes.

13. Cf. R. Pesch, *Das Markus-Evangelium,* Herders theologischer Kommentar zum Neuen Testament, no. 2 (Freiburg, 1976), I:65.

14. According to R. Pesch (op. cit., II:20), the tradition arises before the year 37. He bases himself on the fact that the pre-Markan account speaks of the high priest in office without naming him (Mk 14:53,54,60,61,63). That makes one think that Caiaphas was still in office when the tradition arose (he was the high priest from 18 to 37 A.D.) and is therefore known to all.

15. J. Schreiber sees two original accounts of the crucifixion fused together in Mark. Our text (Mk 15:34) would be part of the second account (vv. 33,34a,37,38), with redactional additions by the evangelist (vv. 34b,35,36,39).

After having criticized this hypothesis, E. Linnemann expounds his own: the motifs of vv. 33 and 38 would be the primitive ones around which our account has been constructed: vv. 33,34a,37,38, to which isolated units were then added: vv. 34b,35,36; v. 39 comes from Mark.

L. Schenke criticizes in turn the hypothesis of Linnemann. According to Schenke, vv. 33 and 38 are later (they come from the Hellenistic community in Jerusalem in polemical discussion with Judaism). The original account would be: vv. 34a,36a,37,39, with secondary additions: vv. 33,34b,38. Vv. 35,36b are redactional.

D. Dormeyer sees vv. 34a,37,38 at the origin of the tradition (the primitive account would have been transmitted under the form of an "account of martyrs"). Mark has added vv. 34b,35,36,39.

For R. Pesch, who insists that Mark is a rather conservative transmitter, the entire text from 14:1 to 16:8 is pre-Markan.

J. Gnilka considers vv. 34a,36a, 37b as primitive. The later additions would be vv. 33,34b,38 and curiously even the cry of v. 37a (an apocalyptic element, according to the author). Vv. 35,36b,39, on the other hand, are redactional.

16. L. Schenke, op. cit., 97.

17. This argument has been invoked above all to show the historicity of the cry of abandonment: "The historical authenticity of this utterance of Jesus is certain enough: it is not a sentence that the Christian community could have attributed to Jesus if he had not uttered it, because the abandonment that it enunciates poses a problem of faith. Of its own initiative, the Christian community would not have put an utterance on the lips of Jesus that at first view would have made a concession to its enemies by affirming the abandonment of the Crucified by God. Only fidelity to the historical testimony could have demanded the presence of this recollection in the redaction of the Gospel," writes J. Galot (*Il mistero della sofferenza di Dio* [Assisi:Cittadella ed., 1975], 47f).

This line of argumentation, however, remains weak. It is necessary, in fact, to situate oneself better in the context of a Jewish community of Palestine. Cf. also W. Trilling, *Christus Verkündigung in den synoptischen Evangelien* (Munich: Kösel-Verlag, 1969), 200.

18. Cf. A. Deissler, "Mein Gott, warum hast du mich verlassen! (Ps 22, 2)," in *Ich will euer Gott werden*, Stuttgarter Bibelstudien, no. 100 (Stuttgart, 1981), 107–109.

19. Op. cit., 106.

20. Cf. L. Ruppert, 50ff; L. Schenke, 97; D. Dormeyer, 31; the comment of J. Gnilka, II:311, etc.

21. The very translation into Greek of the Aramaic words of Jesus in Mark 15:34b favors the antiquity of the cry. This translation was very probably made before the redaction of the Gospel and dates back to the period in which the readers no longer understood the Aramaic language. It could even go back to the Hellenistic community of Jerusalem.

Hence, the conclusion of L. Schenke (p. 96): "One will thus find it difficult to consider v. 34a as a 'secondary interpretation of the wordless cry of v. 37.'"

A further consideration: if only the inarticulate cry (v. 37) were historical and v. 34a a later interpretation, vv. 35–36 would then have to come from the community also, since they presuppose the cry of abandonment of v. 34. But the community would scarcely have invented such a scene, since it never invokes the help of Elijah and would place such a request in the mouth of the Lord even less.

22. "Psalm 22 und das Neue Testament," *Zeitschrift für Theologie und Kirche* 68 (1968):17. On this topic, cf. the study of J. Oswald, "Die Beziehungen zwischen Psalm 22 und dem vormarkinischen Passionsbericht," *Zeitschrift für Katholische Theologie* 1 (1979):53–66.

As the title of the article indicates, the author examines the relations between Psalm 22 and the pre-Markan account of the passion in order to learn what the point of departure of the tradition is and to seek to overcome the dilemma owing to the respective positions of Dibelius and Bultmann. According to Dibelius, in fact, there is the predominant influence of reflection from the Old Testament on the formation of the pre-Markan tradition of the passion.

For Bultmann, on the other hand, at the origin of the tradition are found the announcements of the passion proceeding from the kerygma (cf. Mk 8:31ff) and a brief report of historical recollections which were subsequently amplified.

In short, is there at the origin of the tradition of the passion a reflection that takes its point of departure from the Old Testament or an amplified historical report?

For J. Oswald, this alternative does not exist. He takes into account the characteristic usage of the Old Testament in the pre-Markan account which no longer follows the announcement-fulfillment schema; that is, the events narrated of the passion are no longer seen as a fulfillment of Old Testament episodes.

"In the pre-Markan account of the passion, the events are narrated with Old Testament formulations. The words and idioms from the Old Testament employed by it had as a technical theological language a particular function to perform. By relating the new in the 'colors' of the old, one makes it clear that it is a question of the same thing in the New Testament as in the Old, i.e., the salvific action of God. The idioms borrowed from the Old Testament are inserted into the setting of the account . . . and adapted to the new context. With that it is no longer the Old Testament announcement that determines how the New Testament fulfillment is to look; rather, the events at the crucifixion of Jesus determine in which place the formulations of the Old Testament are to stand" (pp. 61–62).

Moreover, the references to Psalm 22 are found only in the account of the crucifixion; and, what is more, this account utilizes only words and locutions taken from Psalm 22. According to the author, the influence of Psalm 69 on Mark 15:23 is uncertain, and in any case, Mark 15:23 would be a later addition to the pre-Markan text.

How is one to explain the fact that Psalm 22 is to be read only in the account of the crucifixion? Because the behavior of Jesus during the passion—his silence until the last moment, his submission to the will of the Father—did not correspond to the behavior of the psalmist who cries out from the beginning and proclaims his trust in God in a loud voice. Psalm 22 is therefore fitting only from the point of the crucifixion on. It is there that the disciples noticed a certain similarity of the events with the content of the first part of the psalm. "These differences and the fact that explicit references to Psalm 22 are found only in the account of the crucifixion do not permit one to consider this Old Testament text as the origin of the tradition of the passion" (p. 59).

By taking into consideration the characteristic usage of the Old Testament and the fact that in the account of the passion the influence of Psalm 22 is found only in the presentation of the crucifixion, the author arrives at the conclusion that from the beginning of the tradition there existed an indissoluble bond between the historical account and words borrowed from the Old Testament.

"The concordance between the experiences of the disciples and the different affirmations of Psalm 22 have thus led to an account of the passion in which the events are presented in part with sober words and in part with words and idioms of this Old Testament text. Both are seamlessly connected in the narration. . . . The idioms from the Old Testament belong to the account of the passion from the beginning. No rupture is noticeable in the pre-Markan account of the passion between historical narration and Old Testament idiom. Both belong so inseparably close together that we cannot separate them either" (p. 63).

23. "Das letzte Wort Jesu," *Studia Theologica* 17 (1963):111.

24. *Matteo. Commento al "Vangelo della Chiesa"* (Assisi: Cittadella ed., 1973), p. 689, n. 48.

25. The text does not permit one to say that the mockers imitated the cry by referring it to the prophet: "Elijah, Elijah, why have you abandoned me?" (cf. R. Pesch, op. cit., in loco).

26. "Das letzte Wort Jesu," art. cit., 103–119.

27. The idea was already advanced by H. Sahlin, "Zum Verständnis von drei Stellen des Markus-Evangeliums," *Biblica* 1 (1952):62–66.

28. For example, X. Léon-Dufour, *Face à la mort,* 160–162.

29. R. Schnackenburg, op. cit., III:332, n. 67.

30. R. Pesch, op. cit., II:500, n. 495.

CHAPTER 3

The Cry of Abandonment in the Light of the Old Testament

Let us return to the pre-Markan account of the crucifixion and death of Jesus and try to grasp the fundamental motif underlying it and structuring it.

The Recourse to the Old Testament

For the first Christian community, recourse to the Old Testament became necessary from the beginning. Only by means of Scripture was it possible to overcome the scandal of a Messiah who dies on the cross and to penetrate the meaning of that death, whether for the faith itself or to announce the Risen One to the Jewish world.[1]

In fact, reading the crucifixion and the death of Jesus shows that the Old Testament has its importance there.

It is not yet a question of explicit citations but of approximations, of word choices, of discrete allusions, which however cannot escape the attentive reader and which introduce him to a certain understanding of the passion.[2]

This absence of explicit citations indicates that the tradition was not yet interested in finding in the Old Testament messianic texts that prophesy details of the life of the Messiah and show that the crucified Jesus fulfills them. Its intention is to insert the passion of Christ into the important spiritual and theological current of the *suffering servant*.

One notes, in fact, that the choice of Old Testament texts follows a precise line. They are references to the psalms of lamentation, in particular to Psalm 22, or in any case to the texts that speak of the *passio justi,* i.e., of the just man who has to suffer because of his fidelity to Yahweh and feels abandoned by God to adversity. But precisely in this overwhelming experience of the absence of God, the suffering Christ proclaims his trust and certainty that Yahweh will save him.

P. Grelot expresses it thus: "The worst of the sufferings is that of the silence of God. This silence does not place faith in question but inscribes itself as an incomprehensible test within this faith itself."[3]

Such a religious experience, expressed in the Book of Job, in the final songs of the servant of Yahweh (Is 50:4–9; 53), in the interpretation made of it by the Book of Wisdom (Wis 2–5) in the first century B.C., and in numerous psalms of lamentation, certainly constitutes one of the most profound and existential realizations that man is able to have in his relationship with God. It belongs to the fundamental privileges of Israel and to its self-consciousness of its destiny among the nations.

The Suffering Servant: A Theology of Martyrdom[4]

The account of the crucifixion and of the death of Jesus was thus written in the language of the psalms of lamentation and along the lines of the *passio justi.* But the latter, in turn, is understood according to the interpretation it received in Judaism at the time of the rise of the pre-Markan tradition, of which Wis 2–5 is an important witness (even if written first).

In order to obtain a better understanding, it is advisable to follow the evolution of the *passio justi* motif in the Old Testament.

In the ancient psalms of lamentation, the situation of the prayer is presented in vividly graphic terms: he is prey to suffering, feels near to death, and, as in Psalm 22, has a real and painful experience of the absence of God. In particular, this is the case of the sick.

Sickness was in fact understood as a sign of separation from Yahweh. To such a situation it is necessary to add the judgments, the criticisms, even the mockeries of the surrounding persons and of the adversaries who called the innocence of the victim into doubt. These things have the effect of strengthening in the prayer the feeling of abandonment by God and thus put his faith to a severe test. But in spite of all, the victim proclaims his trust in God and expresses the certainty that Yahweh will hear his invocation. God will intervene and heal him, he will save him from his enemies, he will see to justifying him and to showing his rectitude and innocence to the eyes of all.

In the sapiential literature—cf. Psalms 34, 37, 112, 119, and especially Wisdom 2–5—the theme evolves on the one hand as a spiritualization of the *passio justi* motif. One no longer expects an immediate intervention of God on this earth but one's recompense in the beyond (one notes the influence of apocalyptic elements like the resurrection and immortality). Consequently, the persecuted just man refuses to justify himself before his enemies: God himself will do so when in the next life his enemies will take cognizance of their errors. The just man thus accepts the sufferings his adversaries cause him as an aspect of divine pedagogy.

On the other hand, the adversaries in question have become those who spurn the divine law; they persecute the just one precisely because he is faithful to the law and knows himself to be loved by God, chosen by him as a son:

> Let us beset the just one, because he is obnoxious to us;
>   he sets himself against our doings,
> Reproaches us for transgressions of the law. . . .
> He professes to have knowledge of God
>   and styles himself a child of the Lord . . .
>   and boasts that God is his Father.
> Let us see whether his words be true;
>   let us find out what will happen to him.
> For if the just one be the son of God, he will defend him
>   and deliver him from the hand of his foes. . . .

> For if before men, indeed, they be punished,
>   yet is their hope full of immortality;
> Chastised a little, they shall be greatly blessed,
>   because God tried them
>   and found them worthy of himself. . . .
> Then shall the just one with great assurance
>   confront his oppressors. . . .
> Seeing this, they shall be shaken with dreadful fear,
>   and amazed at the unlooked-for salvation.
> (Wis 2:12–13; 16–18; 3:4–5; 5:1–2).

Whereas in the psalms of lamentation the just man was mocked *even though* he was just and in spite of his rectitude, now he undergoes persecution precisely *because* he is just, faithful to the law, and Son of God. The *passio justi* empties into a *theology of martyrdom*. Consequently, the persecutions of the adversaries no longer put his faith to the test; his trust is no longer threatened by doubt. On the contrary, the suffering inflicted becomes the proof of his justice and strengthens the certainty of his rectitude. Instead of confirming the victim in the feeling of abandonment by God, it is in reality the sign of divine election.

The Passion of Christ and the "Passio Justi"

This way of understanding the *passio justi* underlies precisely the account of the passion and death of Christ in the pre-Markan tradition:

• Jesus renounces every sort of self-justification before his enemies.

• He accepts his sufferings even unto death without expecting the intervention of God demanded by his enemies as a sign of his rectitude.

• Jesus, the Just One, awaits the intervention of God not in this life but in death.

• By his whole behavior and especially by the tortures he underwent he shows himself to be the "Son of God."

• God intervenes in his death by resurrecting him. The darkness (v. 33) and the torn veil (v. 38) are the signs of such a divine intervention on behalf of the just man—which corresponds to the answer to prayer in the psalms of lamentation.

It is in this perspective that the earliest community understood the passion and death of Jesus. And the latter's cry—Psalm 22:2—is to be situated in this total context. Without in any way attenuating *a priori* the realism and the harshness contained in the beginning of Psalm 22:2, the pre-Markan tradition saw in the cry of abandonment not a provocation of its own faith but, on the contrary, the proof that Jesus is the Just One, the Son of God.

On the other hand, in a context that presents the just man as one who submits himself to his destiny even unto death, who expects his recompense from God in the beyond, who finds in his very sufferings the certainty of his divine election, the cry of abandonment appears as something unexpected and is placed particularly in the limelight, all the more since in our account of the crucifixion it is the only explicit citation of the Old Testament and at the same time the only utterance of Jesus on the cross. In a context of a theology of martyrdom this cry of abandonment by God finds no place. Even if in other accounts (2 Mc 7; 1 En 95, etc.) the victim does open his mouth, it is to proclaim his fidelity and hope or to launch invectives against his enemies.

It is now necessary to deepen our remarks.

The pre-Markan tradition certainly wishes to insert the tragic end of Jesus into the spiritual current of the *passio justi* and thus to show that the Crucified took upon himself the same experience that many just men had had in the Old Testament.

But is Jesus nothing other than a man unjustly condemned like so many others, a martyr? Does he only extend the list of the numerous suffering servants of Israel? In other words, did the primitive Church wish to proclaim only his innocence?

It knows that the death of Jesus is a unique event, since the One nailed to the cross is the long-awaited Messiah. This characteristic is underscored from the beginning by the connection made in the account of the passion between the theme of the suffering servant and that of the messianic kingship (Mk 15:26; 14:53–15:20).

By placing the destiny of the Messiah in the perspective of the *passio justi,* the young Church effected a theological upset of audacious originality: as the Just One, even the Messiah must undergo the destiny of the just of which Scripture speaks; the Messiah himself must pass through suffering. This final consequence was not foreseen in the messianic expectation of Judaism and could not be explicitly understood from the Old Testament.

The result is surprising: the Christian community was then able to see in the lamentable end of Jesus not the failure of his claim to be the Messiah but the confirmation that he really was so. "All these songs and reflections of the Old Testament," L. Schenke writes, "describe the fate of suffering of the Just One, his persecutions, afflictions, revilements, and deepest humiliations to the point of death. Was this then the lot assigned by God to the Just One? Did God's will consist in letting the Just One suffer before he exalted and glorified him, before he stood by him and conferred on him the dignity that was his? If this was the case, then such a will of God could also hold for the Just One, for the Messiah. Then the fate of Jesus, his fruitless failure on the cross, his apparent abandonment by God says nothing against his being the Messiah."[5]

By this recourse to Scripture, by this understanding of the death of the Messiah, the Church succeeded in overcoming the principal obstacle, the scandal that Jesus and his death constituted for the Jews, and in giving this event its most profound interpretation. There is, in fact, in the event of the cross of Christ an aspect that distinguishes it from the just man persecuted because of his justice by the enemies of God. The enemies who mock the Crucified are the representatives of Israel. Jesus was condemned by observers of the law and in the name of the law.

It is along these lines that the cry of abandonment acquires its full value in the pre-Markan tradition: this cry does not only express the consequence of the suffering endured on the cross as such; it is the rejection itself of Christ by Israel in the name of the law, experienced as the rejection of God. Jesus exits from the covenant of God with Israel. In Pauline terms, he has died through the law to the law (cf. Gal 2:19); he has become a "curse," since "accursed is anyone who is hanged on a tree" (Gal 3:13).

In this theological drama, manifested by the cry of Psalm 22:2, Jesus touches the depths of the trial of the suffering servant of Israel. But at the same time, he overcomes the old covenant and attains the estranged condition of every man before God.

It is self-evident that the theological reflections by means of which the primitive Church integrated the death of Jesus into its understanding of the faith do not at all contradict the possibility that it was the unfolding of the historical facts that drove the community to interpret the account of the crucifixion and death of Jesus in the light of Psalm 22—in other words, that the behavior of Jesus was at the origin of the theological reflection of the community.

But once the theological imprint of the latter upon our account is admitted, one sees what consequences are contained in the affirmation that Jesus is the Messiah who has suffered the fate of the suffering servant and thus in the consideration that his death in the name of the law was willed by God. The cross acquires a definitive value: it is an *eschatological event* (the "darkness" of Mark 15:33), but also an event of *universal* dimensions which overcomes the old economy (the "torn veil" of Mark 15:38).

Notes

1. "In the most ancient form accessible to us, the narration of the passion is not intended to move us but to make us reflect, to permit the reader to find the sense of what is happening. And that can be done only by seeking in the Old Testament the witness to the plan of God. One seeks to master the scandal of the passion—a crucified Messiah!—by interrogating the Word of God. Nor is any other way possible" (J. Delorme, *Lettura del Vangelo di Marco* [Assisi: Cittadella ed., 1977], 172).

2. In the account of the crucifixion we find: Mk 15:24: the dividing of the garments (= Ps 22:19); Mk 15:29: the bypassers shake their heads (= Ps 22:8); Mk 15:34: the cry of abandonment (citation of Ps 22:2); Mk 15:36: the giving of vinegar to drink (= Ps 69:22);

We find possible allusions or references to: Am 8:9 (the cosmic struggle: Mk 15:33); Ps 31 (the insults of the adversaries: Mk 15:29); Is 53 (placement between the evildoers: Mk 15:27); Wis 2:18 (the recognition of Jesus as Son of God: v. 39b).

The diptych of Wisdom 2:12–20; 5:1–7, a sort of commentary that actualizes the song of the servant of Yahweh (Is 53), has played a prominent role.

In the account of Matthew, references to the Old Testament increase: Mt 27:34 = Ps 69:22; Mt 27:43 = Ps 22:9.

3. P. Grelot, *Dans les angoisses l'espèrance* (Paris: Ed. du Seuil, 1983), 222.

4. On this theme: E. Schweizer, *Erniedrigung und Erhöhung bei Jesus und seinen Nachfolgern* (Zurich, 1962); L. Ruppert, *Jesus als der leidende Gerechte?* Stuttgarter Bibelstudien, no. 59 (Stuttgart, 1972). The excellent overview given by Marie-Louise Gubler, *Die Frühesten Deutungen des Todes Jesu*, Orbis Biblicus et Orientalis, no. 15 (Freiburg [Switzerland]: Universitätsverlag and Göttingen: Vandenhoeck und Ruprecht, 1977), 95–205, were very useful to me.

5. Op. cit., 106f.

CHAPTER 4

The Place of the Cry of Abandonment in the Present Account

In the preceding chapter, I tried to present the content of the pre-Markan tradition on the death of Jesus.

Now I should like to take the present text into consideration, the text as Mark wrote it and as we presently read it. I do not claim to grasp the evangelist's own interpretation at the redactional level. In order to do this, it would be necessary to know exactly the additions and revisions that he made on his source. This is not concretely possible, even if one may think with good reason that, at least in the account of the crucifixion and death of Jesus, his contribution was minimal.

It remains to be asked whether Mark was able in addition to discern the profound motifs underlying his source.

In spite of these uncertainties, the cry of abandonment receives a new dimension if one enlarges the immediate context in which it has been read until now.

Abba, the God of the Abandoned

The cry "My God, my God, why have you forsaken me?" acquires a new dimension if it is understood in the perspective of the entire Gospel, the Gospel Mark has entitled "The Gospel of Jesus *Christ, Son of God*" (Mk 1:1).

In the light of his life, of his unique relationship with the Father, and of his announcement of the nearness of the reign of

God, the cry on the cross opens an access to the intimate life of
God himself. The only time the evangelist transmits the Aramaic
appellative, "Abba," with which Jesus usually expressed his personal relationship with God is precisely in the garden of Gethsemani.

The "my God" invoked on Calvary is none other than the
Abba, the God whom Jesus addressed during his earthly existence
with filial trust, with the assurance and tenderness a child has
toward his "Daddy," the Father to whom he knows himself to
owe all. A most unique bond exists between Jesus and his God.

"It is continually reported that Jesus called God 'my Father' in
an exclusive sense. That expresses a communion with God that
is no longer mediated through the covenant, the people, and the
tradition and is thus to be called 'immediate.' It belongs to the
unprecedented claim of Jesus to forgive sins here already with the
divine right of grace. If Jesus identified himself with God in this
way, he must have presupposed that God for his part identified
himself with him and his word. But whoever lived and preached
thus in nearness to God, his kingdom, and his grace and bound
the decision of faith to his person could not have understood his
deliverance to an accursed death on the cross as a mere misfor-
tune, or as a human misunderstanding, or as a final trial. Rather,
he must have experienced it as abandonment by precisely the God
whom he had dared to call 'my Father.' "[1]

The experience of abandonment had by Jesus is, then, something more than the cry of the suffering servant of the Bible. Here
it is a question of the relationship between the Father and the one
whom he calls "my Son, my beloved." It is, then, not enough to
interpret Psalm 22:2 in the light of the Old Testament; one must
give it a new content that proceeds from the reality that Jesus
himself is. "If as he was dying he cries out for God, then he cries
not only for the God of the Old Testament but for the God whom
he called his Father in an exclusive sense and to whom he knew
himself to be bound in a unique way."[2]

Again J. Moltmann: "In the usual interpretation, the cry of Jesus is understood in the sense of the prayer of Psalm 22. But even
if two texts have the same formulation, they do not necessarily

have the same content, which a tradition-critical consideration easily overlooks. It is therefore not correct to interpret Jesus' cry in the sense of Psalm 22; rather, it is more correct to interpret the words of the psalm here in the sense of Jesus' situation. In the original Psalm 22, 'my God' means the God of the covenant with Israel and the 'I' of the abandoned one the covenant partner, the suffering servant. In the case of Jesus, however, the whole content of his own message of the graciously approaching God, who often let him speak in an exclusive sense of 'my Father,' lies in the call 'my God.' . . . It is 'his' God and Father for whom he cries. It is not another God but indeed a special relationship to God with respect to Israel's traditions. On the other hand, the 'I' of the abandoned one is accordingly no longer simply identical with the I of an Old Testament just man faithful to the covenant but must be understood in a special way as the I of the Son."[3]

In the cry of abandonment, does not the account of the passion, indeed the entire theological reflection, come precisely to a turning point?

"It happens on the cross that God the Father lets the one die who claimed to be his Son. Either such a claim was empty, and then the cross can be nothing other than the end of the adventure of the man Jesus; or this claim was well founded, and then the cross is the climax of the revelation of the intimate life of God."[4]

The Place of the Cry of Abandonment in the Passion

The passage in Mark 15:33–39 gives the impression of being constituted by the juxtaposition of small literary units that narrate different events which took place one after the other: the darkness—the cry of Jesus—the mockery of those present—the death of Jesus—the torn veil of the temple—the confession of faith of the centurion at the foot of the cross.

In reality, the interpretation of the text made in the first chapter has shown that the meaning predominates over the chronicle events: everything converges toward the death and serves to give it a dimension of eschatological revelation. Seeing now the place that the cry of abandonment occupies in this context and, more generally, in the account of the passion will permit us to grasp better the importance that it has for the evangelist.

But in order to understand correctly all that will come to light, it is again necessary to give a brief introduction.

Throughout his Gospel, Mark has already prepared the reader for the correct understanding of the death of the Messiah.

He orients the activity of Jesus toward it. But in order to make us understand that Christ is not crushed under the weight of an inevitable fate, the victim of a blind destiny, his way toward the passion is presented under the sign of the divine will: " . . . the Son of Man *had to* suffer much . . . " (Mk 8:31; then 9:31; 10:32ff). The destiny toward which he is freely headed is placed in the will of the Father. Mark thus reveals the reality that moved Jesus: his fidelity to his own message, the obedience to him who is his very existence.

All this becomes particularly explicit at the threshhold of the passion true and proper in the garden of Gethsemani: "Abba . . . let it be as you would have it, not as I" (Mk 14:36). These words of Jesus, which release the unfolding of the passion, are also for the evangelist the key to all that is about to happen, a warning to read all that follows in this light.

Behind the ugly and distressing events that are narrated, there unfolds another story hidden from the eyes of flesh, the story of love between the Son and the Father which culminates paradoxically in the cry: "My God, my God, why have you abandoned me?" In order not to be misunderstood, this cry must be illuminated by the light projected on the entire passion by the words of Jesus said in the garden of Gethsemani.

I shall now return to the theme of this chapter. The fundamental place the evangelist attributes to the cry of Jesus in the context of his death already appears from the fact that it is the *only* utterance of Jesus on the cross. It is not very probable that Mark and the tradition before him transmitted this utterance as one devotedly preserves the words of a deceased loved one. Such a view is already excluded by the very content of the cry. The latter interests the Church on account of its theological weight: an utterance placed in the mouth of Jesus is always a crucial moment for faith.

And, in fact, the cry of abandonment does not come unexpectedly. There is a whole gradation in the series of events that prepare it and introduce it. This gradation is produced through the schema of the "three hours" (Mk 15:25–33): the first three hours (vv. 25–32) are filled by the mockeries of the bypassers, the high priests, and the scribes.

The following three hours, from the sixth to the ninth hour, are full of darkness. The narrator thus creates in the reader the impression of a crescendo that, scanned in terms of these hours, leads to the ninth hour when Jesus cries: "My God, my God, why have you abandoned me?": the darkness that has invaded the entire world penetrates into the heart of Christ.

Such a crescendo can be observed throughout the entire passion. From the beginning, Jesus is presented in a progressive state of denudation and loneliness: during the agony in the garden of Gethsemani, the disciples sleep (Mk 14:37), then abandon him fleeing (Mk 14:50); and Peter denies him publicly (Mk 14:54ff). Even the crowd withdraws from him; it mocks him beneath the cross together with the religious authorities of Israel and the evildoers (Mk 15:29ff). Deprived now even of his garments—which underscores his loneliness even more[5]—the Crucified is completely abandoned.

At this point, Jesus enters into the greatest loneliness imaginable: the experience of the absence of God.

Nailed to a cross, derided by all, he seems to confirm with his cry the unbelief and the point of view of the representatives of Israel: "Let the 'Messiah,' the 'king of Israel,' come down from that cross here and now so that we can see it and believe in him!" (Mk 15:32).

There is no doubt that for the evangelist, as well as for his source, the cry of abandonment is found at the narrative and theological climax of the account of the passion of Jesus.[6]

A further point. The cry of abandonment is connected with Jesus' death itself. That seems to be all the evangelist wishes to suggest.

I have already said that the mention of the ninth hour in v. 34 has an origin different from that named in v. 33. The latter belongs to an either liturgical or apocalyptic schema of "three hours," whereas the ninth hour of v. 34 is the hour of the death of Christ.

The primitive, historical datum is certainly the recollection of the hour of the death of Jesus. It is possible that in the account of the passion, the schema of "three hours" took its point of departure from the report of the ninth hour in v. 34 and was elaborated in function of it.[7]

Thus, Jesus cries: "My God, my God, why have you abandoned me?" at the hour of his death.

Even v. 37, which relates the death of Jesus, seems to run in this direction. In fact, Mark takes up the expression "a loud cry" (which we read already in v. 34 which introduces Psalm 22:2) without, however, specifying if it is a question of a cry different from that of v. 34. It is therefore possible that the evangelist is suggesting that the reader connect v. 37 with v. 34.[8] Jesus then expires uttering the cry of abandonment.

"The access to the death of Jesus is now as ever the interpretive words that Jesus himself speaks: 'My God, my God, why have you abandoned me?' "[9]

Between vv. 34 and 37, it is true, one finds inserted the episode concerning the prophet Elijah, the helper in times of need. The passage appears as a disturbing element which distracts one's attention from the essential. "Elijah is mentioned here twice and precisely at the moment of Christ's death, i.e., at the moment in which the evangelist and the reader should have other concerns!"[10]

Certainly, the episode only confirms the non-intervention of heaven on behalf of the Crucified and thus prolongs the cry of abandonment until his death (v. 37).

But why does Mark preserve vv. 35–36? Let us say that the motive was fidelity to his source. But I do not believe that we betray his intention if we see in the episode something more than an anecdote, if we try to understand it against the background of the Gospel.

I shall hazard a hypothesis. The figure of Elijah has a certain prominence in the Gospel. Nevertheless, only in Mark 15:35–36 does the prophet appear in the guise of a helper of the individual in extreme difficulty. Such a theme is completely foreign to the Christian view, and this speaks in favor of its authenticity.

In the Gospel—and therefore in the Christian tradition—Elijah was always seen in his eschatological function as precursor of the Messiah. The Church—and Jesus first of all—sees this function realized in the figure of John the Baptist. Elijah (John the Baptist) and the Messiah are connected by the divine plan for them in the great eschatological event and by their destiny: the violent death of the Baptist prefigures that of Christ.

It is therefore possible that in the intention of Mark the episode regarding Elijah (Mk 15:35–36) aims at recalling to the mind of the reader the figure of this prophet as he comes to light in the Gospel, particularly in Mark 9:11–13.

In these two texts, the "coming" of Elijah is spoken of, and this reality is put into relation with the death of the Son of Man.

In the following verse (9:13), Jesus declares: "Let me assure you, Elijah has already come. They did entirely as they pleased with him, as the Scriptures say of him." The words of mockery "Now let's see whether Elijah comes to take him down" (15:36b) then appear in all their absurdity. In reality, Elijah and the Messiah are following a divine plan which those present are unable to grasp. It includes the death of the Elect as well as that of the precursor. The episode speaks against those who are mocking him, showing clearly that they understand nothing.

Whatever the case may be, Jesus, uttering a loud cry, expires before the unknown person was able to offer him the vinegar.

The examination of the place of the cry of abandonment in relation to the death of Jesus has led thus far to two conclusions:

• The cry of abandonment should not be understood as an isolated episode, one of so many that preceded the death of Christ. Certainly, we do not have precise historical information in this regard. It is nonetheless important to observe the theological connection that the evangelist sees between abandonment and death.

• In the second place, one cannot consider the cry from a historicizing perspective, i.e., as one simple though certainly excruciating episode among the others that form the plot of the passion.

Mark does not content himself with transmitting an historical recollection. Rather, in it we find on the lips of Jesus himself the interpretation of his passion and death on the cross in its most profound (but not exclusive) aspect.

Let us now tie the loose ends together. The reader cannot escape the impression of total darkness and loneliness caused by the reading of the text. The sober and laconic style of the account of the crucifixion renders all the more impressive the inner and outer denudation, the extreme loneliness to which the dying Jesus attains. He occupies the center of the narration, a center that presents him as abandoned by earth and by heaven, by men and by God. In short, "Jesus' death leaves at first only the impression of a total failure. (. . .) The liberation is lacking."[11]

The Son of God has thus passed through the entire gamut of human anguish. He experienced death in all the tragic religious meaning acquired as a consequence of sin: estrangement from God. He became, as Paul will say, "sin," a "curse" (2 Cor 5:21; Gal 3:13), and that to the extreme consequence of sin: death. The theological dimension of abandonment now comes to light: Jesus, the incarnate Son, has completely assumed the human condition of estrangement from God.

But the reader should not forget Jesus' line of conduct, which the evangelist indicated at the beginning of the passion: "But let it be as you would have it, not as I" (Mk 14:36).

The experience of Christ on the cross is essentially an experience of unity with the Father. That of which the hymn in the Letter to the Philippians sings now appears in all its paradoxical truth: "obediently accepting even death, death on a cross!" (Phil 2:8). Jesus loved in such a way as to experience separation, disunity, abandonment: the loss of God for the love of God.

In the understanding of faith, everything is overturned at once: the extreme abandonment is in reality the fullness of love, the profound loneliness is total unity. At the moment in which he appears forsaken, he is identified more than ever with the divine will; he is transparent to the Father. And in this weakness without end, Jesus finds himself "delivered" without reserve to the Power of the Father, totally open to the creative act of the resurrection.

"As an act of supreme filial obedience (cf. 14:36), the death of Jesus realizes the perfect union of his humanity with God and thus attains to the formation of the new man, perfectly consecrated by the invasion of the Glory of God (cf. Ex 40:34; 1 Kgs 8:10; 2 Mac 2:8): in other words, it attains to the resurrection."[12]

The death on the cross—sign of the divine curse—which seems to crown the total failure of Jesus, inaugurates on the contrary the reversal of the situation. From a sign of curse, the death of the Abandoned becomes a sign of the new, definitive, and universal salvific presence of God.

This reversal of the situation is manifested by two signs, closely connected by the evangelist to the death of Christ: the torn veil (v. 38) and the centurion's confession of faith (v. 39). Two realities are thus signified by Mark, two realities rooted in the death of Jesus experienced in this manner.

• Jesus is the new temple not made by human hands, now the place of the eschatological presence of God.

• His death is the full manifestation for all mankind of his unity with the Father, of his reality as Son.

Thus, in the death, in the total impotence of the One who was derided by the crowd, by the high priests, and by the scribes, who appeared to all as abandoned by God himself, the divine response is unexpected and new: God is totally on the side of the One abandoned by God. He manifests his presence where the man who thinks he knows him does not seek him, indeed proclaims his absence. In his death experienced as abandonment, Jesus himself is the ultimate revelation of the God of Revelation.

Everything suddenly changes its appearance: Israel itself, present at the foot of the cross with its various representatives, expresses through their mockeries its non-comprehension of the event, of the eschatological action of God, and is, as it were, enveloped in the shadow of the old world which has passed away. The divine presence leaves the temple and takes up its dwelling in the body of the Crucified. In the latter, the passage from the old covenant to the new is effected, a passage that is not restoration but absolute innovation.

The reality thus expressed by means of the signs that accompany the death of Christ overcomes the anti-Jewish polemic that sometimes seems to surface in the Gospel (cf. Mk 13:2, etc.). Access to God in Christ is opened to all, Jews and non-Jews; it is open to faith.

In Jesus abandoned and risen, the presence of the God of Israel has crossed the boundaries of the sacred to become universal and to penetrate into the profound miseries of a humanity estranged from God. By refusing Jesus as the Messiah, indeed precisely in that refusal concretized in the crucifixion on the wood of the curse, Israel realizes the divine plan in its regard, which is to bring God to all nations. Certainly, the chosen people expected the Messiah in an entirely different way!

We can follow the thought of the evangelist even further. In order to penetrate more deeply into it, one must take account of the inclusion that exists between Mk 15:38–39 and the declarations of Jesus before the Sanhedrin: Mk 14:58, 61–62. It is not by chance that the themes presented by Mark immediately after the death of Jesus—the veil of the temple and the centurion's confession of faith—correspond to the two important declarations of Jesus that caused his condemnation.[13]

The first declaration—related in the form of an accusation, the only one that is important to the evangelist to write—regards the temple: "I will destroy this temple made by human hands" and "In three days I will construct another not made by human hands" (14:58).

The other declaration, provoked by the high priest, concerns his identity: "Are you the Messiah, the Son of the Blessed One?"

But Jesus says: "I am; and you will see the Son of Man seated at the right hand of the Power and coming with the clouds of heaven" (14:61–62): a particularly solemn affirmation in which Mark concentrates the three great titles, Son of God, Messiah, and Son of Man.

In a certain sense, the passion runs on the rails of these two declarations which will be taken up again in the form of a mockery of the Crucified: "Ha, ha! So you were going to destroy the temple and rebuild it in three days! Save yourself now by coming down from that cross!" (15:29–30) and: "Let the 'Messiah,' the 'king of Israel,' come down from that cross here and now so that we can see it and believe in him!" (15:32).

The cross seems to belie the declarations of Christ and to prove his opponents right. The failure of his claims is led through successive waves of mockeries to the cry of abandonment where the two declarations converge and are annihilated, as it were: God abandons Jesus who claimed to be his Son; he destroys him and not the temple.

"In this oppressive atmosphere, the cry of Jesus, a citation of Psalm 22:2, seems to prove his insultors right. It is not the temple of Jerusalem that is abandoned by God and handed over to destruction but Jesus who spoke against the temple. The humanity of Jesus undergoes a sort of execration in the etymological sense that is opposed to 'consecration.' It is the mystery of the paroxysm of the trial which conditions the perfection of the gift. In reality, this execration flows into the full revelation of the Son of God, as the continuation of the psalm suggests and the Gospel will show. By completely accepting the will of the Father, Jesus manifests himself as the one who is united with the Father in love."[14]

But when everything seems lost, everything begins on another plane. In the death of the one abandoned by God, "it seems that everything is finished in the negative sense of the word, i.e., that everything is annihilated. In reality, everything is finished in the positive sense of the word: everything is fulfilled."[15]

Consequently, Mark takes up again the two themes that have run throughout the passion, but now as signs of glory, as a manifestation of God in Jesus: the temple not made by human hands is nothing other than the glorified humanity of Jesus; in order that it might shine universally with God, it was necessary that his limited carnal condition—the temple made by human hands—be destroyed.

The one whom the high priest declared a blasphemer and whom the crowd derided is now recognized by men as the Son of God. Now, through the experience of the cross and the abandonment, he can truly bear witness both to his unity with the Father and to what the love of God is.

The light shines forth in the darkness. In order to create the new, it was necessary for the old to pass away.

In the light of the leading thread that runs through the entire passion, the place the evangelist attributes to Jesus in his abandonment now appears: it is the focal point and the passageway, the revelation of divine interiority, and the definitive and universal presence of God among men.

Notes

1. J. Moltmann, *Der gekreuzigte Gott* (Munich, 1972), 140f.

2. W. Kasper, *Jesus der Christus* (Mainz, 1974), 140. Cf. also L. Goppelt, *Christologie und Ethik* (Göttingen, 1968), 73.

3. J. Moltmann, op. cit., 142f.

4. P. Ferlay, "Trinité, mort en croix, Eucharistie. Réflexion théologique sur ces trois mystères," *Nouvelle Revue Théologique* 9 (1974):937.

5. According to Jewish symbolism, nudity also expresses the loss of relationship with God. It is, however, possible that the Romans left a piece of cloth on the Crucified in order not to offend the sensibilities of the Jews.

6. Cf. L. Schenke, op. cit., 107.

7. Cf. ibid., 96. On the following page, he writes: "The mention of the 'ninth hour' (v. 34a) is not first of all intended to determine the prayer of Jesus more closely but, rather, his death."

8. Thus Gese, 17; Trilling, 199; Schenke, 97; Boman, 109.

9. D. Dormeyer, op. cit., 88.

10. P. Lamarche, op. cit., 134. The author places the theme of Elijah, which appears frequently in the Gospel, in relation to another important

theme: that of the temple. The allusion to Elijah is also intended to place the unique meaning and newness of the death of Christ into the limelight. According to Malachi 3:1–23, Elijah is to prepare the entrance of the Lord into the temple. The allusion to Elijah thus announces that in death the glorious entrance of Christ into the presence of the Father is about to take place (cf. Mk 16:19) (pp. 134f).

According to Fr. W. Danker, art. cit., 60, Elijah cannot come to Jesus' aid because—according to the tradition taken up by Mark—John the Baptist was Elijah, who had therefore already come.

11. Dormeyer, op. cit., 87.
12. A. Vanhoye, art. cit., 156.
13. Cf. the suggestive analysis of Vanhoye, ibid., 150–156.
14. A. Vanhoye, art. cit., 151.
15. Ibid.

CHAPTER 5

The Historical Panorama

In this chapter I should like to give a brief panoramic view of the interpretations that the cry of abandonment has received in the course of the centuries.

The Fathers of the Church[1]

The cry of Jesus on the cross did not enjoy any particular attention during the patristic era nor in the successive periods of Carolingian and Scholastic theology.

The first to have commented on the text with a certain amplitude was Origen. He finds himself at the beginning of two currents of interpretation that persist until the Middle Ages:

The allegorical interpretation: it is the humanity of men that cries out its anguish through Jesus. The latter as the representative of humanity expresses a reality that does not regard him directly but concerns his body, of which he is the head.

> Taking upon himself our folly and our sins, he cited the words of the psalm: "My sins separate me from my salvation" (PG 12, 1254).

The allegorical interpretation tends to underscore the connection that exists between Christ and men in the work of redemption. Hence, the importance of the idea of solidarity and of substitution:

> He had to submit himself to the abandonment that our human nature had suffered. . . . Then, living like one of the abandoned

73

and also participating like us in flesh and blood, he says: "Why
have you abandoned me?" writes Cyril of Alexandria (PG 76,
1358).

This current was followed by the majority of Greek and Latin
Fathers. St. Augustine became its most trenchant spokesman.
After having cited the second part of the first verse of Psalm 22,
which the Latin version (and the Greek of the Septuagint) had
translated "Far from my salvation (are) the words of my sins,"
the doctor continues:

> Seeing that Christ certainly is without sin and without guilt,
> should we answer that these (final) words are those of the
> psalm? It would be very incomprehensible and contradictory if
> this psalm were not applied to Christ. And why did the Lord
> himself from atop the cross pronounce the first verse of this
> psalm with his own mouth and say: "My God, my God, why
> have you abandoned me?" What did he wish to make us un-
> derstand if not that the entire psalm refers to him, since he him-
> self pronounced its beginning?
>
> Therefore, there is no doubt that the following words, where
> he says "the words of my sins," are those of Christ. But whence
> then come the sins if not from the body which is the Church?
> The one speaking is thus the body of Christ and the head.[2]

The text of Augustine clearly reveals to us the difficulty found
at the origin of the allegorical interpretation of the cry of abandonment. It is due to the erroneous translation made by the Septuagint and by the Latin version (including the Vulgate) of the
second part of Psalm 22:2. In the Hebrew original one reads:
"Far from my salvation, the words that I cry" (interpretable in
different ways). The Greek translates: "Far from my salvation,
the words of my sins." Since sins cannot be attributed to Christ,
the cry of Jesus is referred to his body, to the Church, or to humanity.

Origen, however, is also familiar with a more literal interpretation: the cry of Jesus on the cross expresses his condition as a

"servant." He finds himself submitted to all the suffering and abandonment such a condition entails:

> It is not licit to believe that he lied when he said: "Why have you abandoned me?" There are those who, because of a certain scruple with regard to Jesus and because they are unable to explain what it means that Christ was abandoned by God, think and say: "What was said is true, but it was said out of humility." On the contrary, we see him who was constituted in the form of God descend from such greatness and abase himself by taking on the form of a servant (Phil 2:7). In all this we see the will of the one who sent him for such a mission. Through this we understand that with respect to the condition in which he was— i.e., the form of the invisible God and image of the Father—he was abandoned by the Father when he took the form of a servant, and abandoned to the station of men to take upon himself such an onerous condition and to meet his death, a death on the cross, which seems to be the most shameful among men.
>
> In fact, the climax of his abandonment takes place when they crucified him and, in order to mock him, placed above his head an inscription that said: "This is Jesus, king of the Jews." The height of his abandonment was also the fact that he was crucified among thieves and that the bypassers insulted him, shaking their heads. . . . Thus, one can understand clearly what the words "Why have you abandoned me?" mean when one compares the glory he had with the Father with the ignominy that he did not avoid facing in order to bear the cross.[3]

This second current admits a situation of real abandonment experienced by Jesus, but it is due to the human condition and its consequences, which he voluntarily assumed, and not to a direct act of the Father. The abandonment is understood as the final, culminating act of abasement which the Son experienced in the incarnation, according to the perspective of the hymn in Philippians 2:6–8.

This interpretation was also taken up by the Fathers of the

Church. In his *Commentary on the Gospel of Matthew,* Jerome condenses it in these terms:

> Do not be amazed at the humility of the words and of the laments of abandonment when, knowing the nature of a servant, you attend to the scandal of the cross.

Athanasius combines the two types of interpretation:

> When he said: "My God, my God, why have you abandoned me?" he spoke for us. For, having taken the nature of a servant and made himself similar to a man and appearing as a man, he humiliated himself, becoming obedient unto death on a cross. . . . But it was not he who was abandoned by God: it was we. For us who were abandoned he came upon the earth (PG 27, 987).

Arianism and Nestorianism which, among other things, utilized the cry of the Crucified to confirm their respective theses (creaturehood of the Word, double personality of Christ) obliged the Fathers to reflect further on the utterance of Jesus on the cross. One now begins to reason from the two natures in Christ: Jesus suffered insofar as he was a man, not as the Word.[4]

A certain number of the Fathers, especially those of the school of Antioch (Eusebius of Cesarea, Epiphanius), but also Hilary of Poitiers and Ambrose of Milan, thought that the cry expressed the separation of the divinity and humanity in Jesus. The "my God, why have you abandoned me?" would not be addressed to the Father but to the Word himself when he abandons the body of the dying Jesus.

> . . . while these things were happening, these words were addressed in the name of his human nature to the divine nature united to it (Epiphanius, PG 15, 1929).[5]

This opinion was contested by others. Thus Theodoretus:

(Christ) who had committed no sins says he has been abandoned and must undergo death, which had acquired power over sinners.

By abandonment, he understands not the separation of the divine nature which was united to him, as some have maintained, but the permission granted (so that) the passion (might take place) . . . " (PG 80, 1010).

The sense that Theodoretus gives to the abandonment of Christ comes close to the sense that philological analysis attributes to the verb itself (in Hebrew and in Greek), a sense that P. Foresi summarizes in these terms: "to leave someone entirely in a precarious situation."[6] The Father abstains from intervening in a situation of suffering provoked by men. This is already the sense that Tertullian gave to the abandonment of Jesus when he wrote that the Father "abandoned him in the sense that he delivered him up (to his adversaries)" (PL 2, 219).

In summary, the Fathers of the Church beginning with Origen are familiar with both an allegorical interpretation of the cry of abandonment and a more literal interpretation which they develop according to different points of view: the abandonment reflects his condition as a servant, it expresses the separation of the divinity of the Word who leaves the body of the Crucified, it regards only his human nature, it means the non-intervention of the Father who delivers Jesus up to his adversaries.

The last two understandings especially are taken up and deepened by Scholasticism. They will then receive the formulation that will remain classic in the Church.

Scholasticism

For Scholasticism, the problem is to know how to reconcile the beatific joy that could not abandon the Lord with the anguish he experienced in the passion. But their attention is concentrated on the agony of Gethsemani; the abandonment is not forgotten, yet it is not the object of a special interest.

Thomas Aquinas speaks of it in the Catena aurea, in his commentary on Psalm 21 (= 22) in which he takes up the allegorical interpretation of the Fathers, in the commentary on the Gospel of Matthew, and in a few rare texts of the third part of the Summa Theologica (q. 47, a. 3; q. 50, a. 2). The first preoccupation of the Angelic Doctor is to circumscribe the precise sense of the verb "to abandon," which means that God does not protect Jesus from his enemies. God exposes him to the passion. The abandonment on the part of the Father thus regards neither the union of Christ with God nor the absence of grace.

In this respect Scholasticism also renders the doctrine of the two natures of Christ more precise. Suffering touches the incarnate Word in his body and in his soul, but only in the soul insofar as it is connected with the senses of the body. Insofar as it is in contact with the beatific vision, the soul of Jesus cannot suffer. One can speak of an inferior and a superior part of the soul of Christ provided that one does not divide an essentially simple reality into two: it is always the same soul whether it applies itself to earthly or heavenly realities.

Jesus was therefore able to be blessed and to suffer at the same time.[7] He could thus suffer all the terrors caused by his adversaries without God's intervening to protect him and still not lose the beatific vision and the joy inherent in it. For its part, the non-intervention of God should not be considered as an act of cruelty but seen in view of the salvation of humanity.

The Rhineland Mystics of the Fourteenth Century

An important turning point in the understanding of the cry of the crucified Jesus is noticeable in the great current of saints and mystics from the Middle Ages, beginning with the Rhineland mystics who first "established a relation between mystical experiences of the absence of God and the cry of the cross."[8] Tauler of Strasbourg "becomes the father . . . of a very widespread theology of the cross that exercized its influence in all the countries of Europe and in the great Orders (Dominican, Jesuit, Carmelite, etc.)."[9]

Christian Duquoc thus presents this new interpretation: "Christ is no longer so much condemned and crucified by men as abandoned by God. And this abandonment is due to 'purifications' that are necessary if one is to approach God. 'He became sin for us,' he underwent the *via dolorosa* that leads from sin to God."[10]

In the sermon for the second Sunday after Easter, Tauler utilizes the image of winter to speak of that

> from which the spiritual man suffers who is truly devoted to God, whom he seeks and pursues in his intention and in his love, avoiding sin with all his strength. But at the same time he is abandoned by God with regard to all sensible devotion. He remains in a great aridity, in a great darkness, in a great coldness, no longer tasting the least sweetness or the least consolation. Our Master suffered this winter for all when in his painful passion he was abandoned by his Father and by his divinity. Certainly, it was naturally united to him, but nonetheless, with regard to the succor that he was entitled to receive, he was abandoned to the point that in all his anguishes, in all his pains, in all his ineffable torments, his weak humanity crushed on all sides by affliction did not receive the least drop of divine consolation or the least succor. . . . It is by considering their thus abandoned Master that all those friends privileged by God should overflow with joy and exultation in the depths of their hearts when they feel themselves to be capable of inwardly following their Pastor whose sheep they are in his total abandonment and his humble resignation.
>
> Happy! Yes, thrice happy are those who will have been able to follow their Pastor and Master so faithfully, bearing without any sort of consolation the winter of abandonment, the abandonment of creatures, and much more the abandonment itself of God. There is no doubt that they will then have God present in themselves in a truer and more useful way than in all of the

exquisite pleasures they could ever find and, if I may say so, in all the springs and summers of the soul.[11]

The difference from the preceding interpretations appears clearly. In the thought of the mystics, the abandonment of Christ on the cross does not consist only in a non-intervention of God on behalf of the Messiah left to the mercy of his adversaries but in an act of God who seems to withdraw and who inflicts a feeling of abandonment upon the soul of Christ. Jesus enters into the "night" of God. The bond that united him to the Father during his life seems to be entirely broken. In fact, it is a question of a feeling on the level of the psyche. In reality, on the other hand, the Father always remains united to Jesus who suffers the abandonment.

These mystics and spiritual authors tend, then, to apply to the crucified Jesus, who cries out his abandonment, the mystical experience of the "dark night" (John of the Cross) which they themselves had. Thus, the abandonment was understood as a stage of the spiritual journey that leads to union with God. Because he took our sins upon himself, Christ is its protagonist. He is consequently the *model*[12] to be imitated and followed on the road that leads to union with God. We have seen this in the sermon of Tauler. Here is an example taken from F. Suso:

> What a delicious thing it would be to know oneself completely abandoned in every abandonment, in all the ways our dear Lord was boundlessly abandoned! He was utterly abandoned, more than any creature was ever abandoned. He cried out: "My God, my God, why have you abandoned me?" And he was abandoned until all was fulfilled and he said: "*Consummatum est.*" It is precisely in this way that man should abandon himself absolutely to God in every suffering, in every desolation.[13]

The same current of thought is developed in Spain with John of the Cross. In the *Ascent of Mount Carmel,* he writes:[14]

Since I have said that Christ is the way and that this consists in dying to nature in what pertains to sense and to the spirit, I now wish to make you understand how this can happen by imitating the examples of Christ, our model and our light.

In the first place, it is certain that Jesus died, spiritually in life and naturally in death, to everything that falls under the domain of the senses, since, as he himself said, he did not have a place to lay his head in life (Mt 8:20) and even less in death.

In the second place, it is evident how at the moment of his death he was also crushed in his soul without any relief or comfort, having been left by the Father according to the inferior part of the soul in an inner aridity so great that he was constrained to cry out: "My God, my God, why have you abandoned me?" That was the most distressing abandonment he had experienced in the senses during his life, and precisely while he was oppressed by it he performed the most marvelous work of all those he had performed in heaven and on earth during his earthly existence, rich in miracles and prodigies, a work that consists in having reconciled and united the human race to God by grace. That took place in the moment in which our Lord attained his greatest humiliation in every field: in the reputation of men who, seeing him die, instead of esteeming him made fun of him; in nature, with regard to which he humiliated himself by dying; in the spiritual help and comfort of the Father, who abandoned him in that moment so that he might pay our debts to the last cent and unite man with God . . . " (Bk. 2, chap. 7, par. 9–11).

The abandonment of Jesus refers, then, to the "night of the spirit" which concerns the inferior part of the soul, according to the traditional doctrine of Scholasticism. This experience of the cross is an essential moment in the work of redemption: it is there, in fact, that Christ unites to God the men whose estrangement from God he took upon himself. The redemption is understood according to the typical view of these mystics (even if the juridical element of a debt to be paid is not lacking): as an ascetical way toward God in which Christ withdraws himself from all that is human, i.e., from all that is considered as a reality that separates one from God. In this view, the abandonment of Jesus is the climax of the redemption: totally denuded, Christ enters into full union with God.

One sees here the relation to Rhineland mysticism but also the more theological imprint of John of the Cross.

Without a doubt, the "mystical" interpretation of the cry of abandonment does not correspond to the results of the present exegesis of Mark 15:34 or Matthew 27:46. We are in the presence of the projection of the spiritual experience of these mystics onto the biblical text rather than in that of an interpretation of the cry of the Crucified. In fact, "the abandonment (on the cross) is not a 'mystical trial,' it is the distress of the just man, delivered to the persecutions of his enemies, whom God apparently no longer remembers since he does not protect him."[15] And Ch. Duquoc is right in defending this conclusion of the study by Carra de Vaux Saint-Cyr against the reproach of "unpardonable superficiality" made by Urs von Balthasar, who is favorable to the "mystical" interpretation.

Nevertheless, I do not believe it fitting to discard the thought of these mystics too hastily. The concept that Duquoc has of the "suffering servant" seems to me a bit narrow if applied as such to Jesus. For him, the just man's experience of abandonment is provoked by the scandal of a God who does not intervene on behalf of the just man to re-establish him in his rights according to the promises made to Abraham and transmitted by the prophets. In reality, it is necessary to take account of the problem of relationship to God already in the Old Testament, especially in the case of a just man who is "sick." The interpretation, then, of the cry of abandonment in the present Gospel of Mark—relationship of love between Son and Father—will confirm that the mystics are at least right in not reducing the sense of the abandonment of Christ to its philological content of a simple non-intervention of God. It would be advisable for contemporary theological reflection to occupy itself seriously with the richness of mystical experiences. The motive for official theology's lack of interest, according to Urs von Balthasar, lies in the fact "that, on the one hand, the implicit theology of the saints is in every case limited to a particular 'affective' or 'spiritual' theology and that, on the other, it remains trapped in the anthropocentric schemas of ascent and purification that still predominate even in the doctor of the Church, John of the Cross."[16]

To conclude this section, let us note the displacement of accent in relation to Scholasticism. The latter tried to resolve the problem of reconciling in the soul of the Crucified the disturbance caused by the sufferings of the passion with the beatific joy that could not cease. For the mystics, it is a question of knowing how to reconcile the permanent unity of Christ with the Father with the feeling of abandonment by God that this same Father inflicts directly on Jesus.

The Reformers: Luther and Calvin

The thought of the first Reformers is in part situated in the preceding spiritual current: the abandonment of Christ is understood as an act of God himself with regard to his Son and not as a simple non-intervention.

Moreover, we again find the idea of solidarity and of substitution which were already present in the allegorical interpretation of the cry with the Fathers of the Church (and afterward). But now it is particularly underscored under the influence of Pauline texts, such as 2 Corinthians 5:21 and Galatians 3:13, in which the apostle writes that Christ became "sin" and a "curse" for us—hence the affirmation that Jesus has undergone in our place the punishment that God in his anger inflicts on the impious. A juridical view of the redemption that places the penal character of the passion and thus of the abandonment in relief now begins to predominate strongly: the abandonment is seen as a punishment that Jesus undergoes in our place. Commenting on Psalm 22 in his *Operationes in psalmos, 1519–1521,* M. Luther writes:

> Christ was and remains just and did not commit any sins. . . .
> But at the moment in which he suffered, he took upon himself
> everything that is ours as if it were truly his, suffering even for

that which we should have borne because of our sins and which the damned already suffer. . . .

The punishment of God which strikes because of sins is not only the pain of death but also the fear and the horror of the troubled conscience which experiences the eternal wrath and is as if it were eternally abandoned and driven far from the face of God . . . (p. 603).

In the eyes (of God) also, Christ was like one abandoned, one accursed, a sinner, a blasphemer, one damned, even if he is without sin and without guilt. The fact that he says "you have abandoned me" is certainly not a joke, a game, or hypocrisy. He is truly abandoned in all, as is the sinner when he sins . . . (p. 605).

A threshold has been crossed that the Rhineland mystics refrained from crossing: placing Jesus directly under the anger and vindictive justice of God expressed in the cry of abandonment, a cry that shows that Jesus would have suffered the pains of the damned in his soul, i.e., would have had the experience of hell.

As one can see, the abandonment experienced by the Crucified is not reduced to a feeling. It does not correspond to a darkening of the psyche in its relationship to God, a work of this very same God. It is a question rather of a real abandonment, a punishment of God in his wrath, even if at bottom this abandonment remains provisory, an act of justice performed on an innocent man who has taken the place of the truly guilty.

Calvin accentuates this line once again:

Not only was his body delivered up for our redemption, but . . . there is another more worthy and more excellent price, that of having suffered the terrible torments that the damned and lost have to feel. . . . Nevertheless, by that we do not wish to infer that God was ever against or angry with his Christ. . . . But we do say that he bore the weight of the vengeance of God insofar as he was stricken and afflicted by his hand and experienced all the signs that God shows to sinners when he becomes angry with them and punishes them.

On the same page, Calvin writes again:

> One cannot imagine a more terrible abyss than feeling neglected
> and abandoned by God, not receiving help from him when he
> is invoked, and expecting only that he has sworn to ruin and to
> destroy us. Now, we see that Jesus Christ came to such a point:
> he was constrained, so much did his anguish weigh upon him,
> to cry out: "My God, my God, why have you left me?"[17]

The connection is thus established between Jesus' cry of abandonment—the Pauline affirmation of Christ's having become
"sin" for us—and the suffering of the damned as punishment for
sins.

The abandonment expresses the moment in which the torments
reach their climax: "One cannot imagine a more terrible abyss,"
Calvin comments. Hell best expresses the enormity of the torments that the damned have to undergo as a punishment for their
sins. The juridical view of the redemptive work which insists on
the penal aspect has remained in a more or less attenuated or
completed form in many Catholic and Protestant theologians up
until the present: Christ takes our place and undergoes the punishment that should have been ours.[18]

The French School of the Seventeenth Century

The presentation of the scene becomes sentimental in the French
orators of the seventeenth century. By way of example, we give
this excerpt from a sermon of Bourdaloue cited by Ch. Duquoc:[19]

> This dereliction and this abandonment by God are in some way
> the pain of damnation that Jesus had to experience for us
> all. . . . It is on Calvary . . . that his vindictive justice acts freely
> and without constriction. . . .
> All that the damned will suffer is only a half-vengeance for
> him. That grinding of teeth, that moaning and wailing, those

fires that can never go out—all this is nothing or almost nothing in comparison with the sacrifice of the dying Jesus Christ.

This was a customary rhetoric of the times used to inculcate the idea of a superlative suffering and to strike the imagination. Along the same lines, it was also said that all the greatest pains and tortures of this earth taken together do not equal a single drop of the sufferings of hell. The abandonment of the Crucified thus lies at the top of this scale.

For Bossuet, God withdrew, so to speak, into one part of the soul of Jesus abandoning

> all the rest to the blows of divine vengeance. God gave vent to his anger; he struck his innocent Son who struggled against the wrath of God.

Louis Chardon is accustomed to translating the cry of abandonment in these terms: "Judge! judge! why has he abandoned me?"[20] Among other things, he writes:

> . . . thus one must conclude that there never was and never will be a subject on whom God has poured out the effects of his anger with greater severity. God, the heavenly Father, avails himself of executioners and demons to accomplish the outward martyrdom of his Son, while he reserves being the immediate cause of his inward passion for himself (p. 155).

For Chardon, it is true, this inner torment touches only the inferior part of the soul of Jesus. The superior part remains in an "excess of joy" as befits the Son of God by nature (p. 156).

Duquoc notes how much the perspective has been displaced in the interpretation of the cry of abandonment and of the passion in general: the cry is no longer that of the just man whom God abandons but of the sinner whom God rejects. One ends up forgetting the innocence of Jesus to such a point that the latter is identified with sinners.

The oratorical and at the same time romantic aspect of this interpretation of the abandonment is too garish. But this is not the most difficult side to accept in this way of seeing things. How are we to understand that God could enjoy the murder of an innocent man? How can we admit that Pilate and the Sanhedrin condemn Jesus in the name of the Father? How can we suppose that God could fictitiously cease loving his Son?[21]

Conclusion

These exaggerations can be understood by placing them in the global framework of the Christian religiosity of these past centuries which was pervaded by a pessimism that reaches its climax in the sixteenth to seventeenth centuries: pessimism with regard to man, a sinner from birth with scant possibilities of being saved; pessimism with regard to God, seen not in his aspects of love and mercy but of severity and vengeance.[22]

Undoubtedly, in these centuries there was an evolution toward the tragic, and the conception of the abandonment of Jesus on the cross shows traces of it: from an abandonment understood as leaving one to the mercy of one's adversaries, as a non-intervention of God, one ends up seeing there the fury of a God thirsty for vengeance with regard to his own Son. The liberty, for example, that these authors take in relating our verse is significant: "Judge" instead of "my God," an exclamation point instead of a question mark, etc.

Many factors have been influential here. "A God who is more of a judge than a Father in spite of the mercy that is credited to him by chance, a divine justice assimilated to a vindictiveness, the conviction that in spite of the redemption the number of the elect will remain small since all humanity has merited hell because of original sin, the certainty that every sin injures and insults God, the rejection of every distraction and of every concession to nature because they distance one from salvation—all these elements

... refer to a 'Christian neurosis,'" a collective neurosis of guilt.[23]

In the presence of such a tragic conception of sin and of the severity of God, the destiny of Jesus on the cross will be all the more strongly threatened by it:

> God, the Father, abandons him, delivers him to the fury of the Jews, treats him as the most abominable of men; and after an infinity of opprobrium, ignominy, and suffering, without any regard for the fact that it is his Son, he has him die by means of the most shameful and cruel execution there ever was. . . . God exercises his vengeance upon him, as if he were in no way related to him. Is it possible that sin is so horrible as to cover the Son of God with horror and to render him abominable in the eyes of this tender Father?[24]

Jesus on the cross no longer has anything before him but a God who is thirsty for vengeance and demands the death of the Son to calm his anger. Certainly, this view deserves to be toned down, and Jean Delumeau has done it very well. There are, of course, exceptions, but on the whole it corresponds to the reality of preaching of that time which looked above all to convert the sinful Christian through fear.

The Experience of Hell: Moltmann, Urs von Balthasar

I shall now leave aside these excessive interpretations of the cry of abandonment in order to dwell on an aspect that merits being looked at more closely: the experience of hell.

This point has been taken up and deepened by modern theologians like J. Moltmann and Urs von Balthasar. It is true that the notion of hell is no longer that of Calvin or of the Orators of the seventeenth century. Today, the view of a rather "affective" theology where hell expresses the maximum of torments has been surpassed. Hell is considered as a theological magnitude that sheds light on the state of death, of estrangement from God, of the absence of salvation, of the failure characterized by the situation of sin in which man lives and dies.

The belief that in his death Jesus had passed through the nether world or reign of the dead in all its dimensions is a well-known doctrinal point in the Church, since it belongs to the content of the Creed—the descent into the netherworld—based on 1 Peter 3:19: Jesus preached (salvation) to the dead. The experience of the netherworld on the part of Christ is generally placed between Good Friday and Easter Sunday according to the liturgical perspective. The originality of Luther and Calvin—who in this are close to the mystics—is to have placed the experience of the *poena damni* not on Holy Saturday but in the state of abandonment by God experienced by Jesus which manifests his death as a death similar to that of the reprobate.

Whatever may be the real value of such a theology of the cross, it was unfortunately often marred by a no longer tenable theology of redemption: it is the "God of vengeance" who hurls his anger against Jesus who suffers the pains of the damned in our place.

The idea that the experience of hell is descried in the cry of abandonment also finds a consensus among modern theologians who are faithful to the perspective of Lutheran theology.

I shall cite J. Moltmann who not only sees in the cry the subjective experience of abandonment had by the Crucified but also introduces this abandonment into the relationship between Father and Son within the Trinity itself. What happens on the cross is an event that primarily regards the life between the divine persons.

> What happens between Jesus and the Father in the abandonment or surrender of Jesus on the cross? The Father "abandons" his "own" Son and rejects him. He whose kingdom Jesus had announced as "imminent" becomes an abandoning God. The Son dies from the curse of the Father; he is the abandoned God; he suffers death in abandonment. The Father however suffers the death of his Son in the pain of his love. The Son suffers the abandonment of the Father whose law of grace he had an-

nounced. The Father suffers the abandonment of the Son whom he had chosen and loved. . . . If the Father acts upon his own Son through a surrendering abandonment, if the Son suffers the abandoning surrender of the Father, then the death on the cross stands between God and God. It stands in the being of God himself between the Father and the Son and totally divides the Father from the Son through the curse. But—taking Romans 8:32 and Galatians 2:20 together—because the Son also surrenders himself and, as Gethsemani shows, accepts the cup of abandonment, both act and suffer together in the surrender, and the cross brings the Son with the Father into the perfect communion of will which is called love. . . . On the cross, Jesus and his God and Father are most deeply divided through the death of the curse and most intimately united through the surrender. From this happening between Father and Son, the surrender itself proceeds, the Spirit, who accepts the abandoned, justifies the godless, and brings the dead to life.

The abandoning God and the abandoned God are one in the Spirit of self-surrender. The Spirit proceeds from the Father and the Son, for he springs from the *derelictio Jesu*.[25]

There would be various things to clarify in the theology of Moltmann, and criticisms are not lacking: how are we to explain a separation in the being itself of God and not only in the God-man relationship with which the Word stands in solidarity? There is certainly a danger of bitheism here, of a split in God, and all the more so since the reality of the Spirit does not have much prominence in the thought of the author. One has to ask: "Does Moltmann not abandon himself to an imaginary, even mythological construction when he declares that there is an 'enmity,' a dissent between the Father and the Son? He speaks of 'God against God,' thus introducing a struggle into God that is difficult to reconcile with the love of the Father and the perfect acceptance by the Son with regard to him from whom he ceaselessly receives himself."[26]

Certainly, the thought of Moltmann is subject to discussion on various, even fundamental points, but in the development of a theology of the cross adequate to the exigencies of the contemporary world, one must come to terms with him.

In any case, the author remains self-consistent when in a radical way he places the suffering of hell in God himself, i.e., in that intratrinitarian "separation" between Father and Son which took place in the abandonment on the cross. "Only if all destruction, all abandonment by God, absolute death, and immersion into nothingness are found in God himself will union with this God be eternal salvation, never-ending joy, sure election, and divine life."[27]

On Catholic terrain, among the more noted theologians, H. Urs von Balthasar sympathizes with the idea of an experience of hell had by Christ. But, following the more accepted tradition, he again places the fullness of such an experience in the "descent into the netherworld" of Holy Saturday. Christ could enter into hell only as a "dead" man, thus on Holy Saturday and not in the "subjective-active experience of the passion." "The utter disarmament of principalities and powers (Col 2:14f), the definitively effective invasion of the strong man's house in order to fetter him (Mk 3:24), the depotentiation of the 'gates of hell' (Mk 16:18): all that can take place only from within, in participation in the absolute passivity of death."[28]

I shall synthesize his thought.[29]

According to the Old Testament conception, Sheol represents the realm of the dead. It is the situation of every man—just or impious—who cannot attain God alone, since every man dies a sinner.

The point of departure lies in the affirmation of faith that Christ died for all men and not only for the elect. In order that salvation may be offered to all in their condition of death, Christ had to penetrate into all the depths of hell and to contemplate "the pure substantiality of hell as 'sin in itself' " ("Mysterium paschale," p. 247).

Christ's solidarity with us is carried to its extreme consequences. "As much as the experience of death might have contained an inner overcoming and thus a triumph over the opposed powers, so little need anything have been experienced subjectively: for this would have abrogated the law of solidarity. Do not forget that among the dead there is no living communication. Here solidarity means being alone with others" ("Mysterium paschale," p. 241).

"The existence of the Redeemer with the dead, or, better, with that death which first makes the dead really dead, is the ultimate consequence of the redemptive commission he received from the Father. It is thus an existence in the most extreme obedience, and, since it is the obedience of the dead Christ, it is theologically the only existing 'obedience of a corpse' (the expression comes from Francis of Assisi)" ("Mysterium paschale," p. 248).

"In this sense, the Son thus considers his own work also in the absolutely anti-divine: in an objective 'triumph' (Col 2:15) that is unimaginably far from every feeling of victory. It is 'glory' at the extreme opposite of 'glory' because it is blind obedience at the same time: having to obey the Father where the last trace of God appears lost (in pure sin) and of every other communication (in pure loneliness)" (*Herrlichkeit,* III/2:216).

This journey (= experience) to the dead, into the hell of their loneliness and estrangement from God, acquires the character of a "confiscation." "Through his unique experience" Jesus becomes "the true possessor of what is called 'hell' in the New Testament. He becomes the judge who has experientially measured all the dimensions of man and can now eschatologically mete out to each one his lot. From this perspective, we thus see the concepts of hell, purgatory, and heaven arise for the first time in a theologically meaningful way" (*Herrlichkeit,* III/2:216).

This, then, is the theological thought of Urs von Balthasar, simplified to the extreme, on the "descent of Christ to the netherworld."

In general, however, one observes a certain reluctance among modern exegetes and theologians to attribute the meaning of an experience of hell to the cry of abandonment of the Crucified.

J. Guillet writes that one cannot read into Mark 15:34 "the cry of a suffering that would be that of the damned. The damned cannot say 'my God': God is only a stranger to him. The most profound dereliction of Jesus remains a prayer."[30]

Martelet also shows himself suspicious with regard to Urs von Balthasar: "We do not follow this important theologian on this point, since hell . . . is the world of absolute refusal of Love."[31]

Without a doubt, there is a problem of language to be clarified. What is meant by "hell"?

If by this term one understands—correctly—the eternalized act of rebellion against Love, of refusal of salvation, one cannot attribute it to Jesus. He was made "sin," but he did not become a sinner. His experience of "hell"—understood as the absence of God characteristic of the situation of sin—was lived in extreme obedience to the Father who sends his Son into the world: and this is paradise.

One can then take as a point of departure, as Urs von Balthasar does, the Old Testament concept of Sheol or the realm of the dead, the realm of darkness where one is unable to praise God, the realm of man estranged from God, since "all men have sinned and are deprived of the glory of God" (Rom 3:23). St. Thomas speaks thus: "Before the coming of Christ, all descend into hell after death, including the holy fathers."[32]

Hell (or the netherworld) before Christ—a theological datum not to be understood chronologically—is thus the place where the just who will welcome the salvation of Christ and the impious who will refuse it dwell in a common remoteness from God and in the impossibility of attaining him with their own strength.

But in order that salvation may be offered *to all*, Jesus, in his journey to the dead, in his experience of death, not only reaches the just who will accept the offer of salvation but also bears the pain of the impious—in the loss of all spiritual light of faith, hope, and love (Urs von Balthasar)—in order to reach even those who will refuse.

He thus runs through all the dimensions of hell so that every man in his estrangement from God will have the possibility of recognizing himself in Christ.

The hell of the damned true and proper comes into being with the coming of Christ, in the "eschatological" decision to refuse his salvation, whereas Sheol, as man's impossibility of attaining communion with God, disappears.

Because he was without sin, because he was sent by the Father, Jesus does not undergo hell as prison from which it is impossible to escape. In the "descent" of Christ, the prison of hell is transformed into a "way." For this reason, as again Urs von Balthasar notes, the Fathers of the Church often present the descent of Christ to the netherworld as a triumphal march: "Today he has entered as a king into prison, today he has burst open the doors of bronze and the fetters of iron. He who was swallowed up like a common man in death has laid waste to hell in God" (Proclus of Constantinople).

Hell—like paradise—is now the possession of Christ. It is again St. Thomas who underscores this aspect: "In fact, one triumphs perfectly over another when one defeats him not only on the field but also when one invades his very house. Now, Christ had triumphed against the devil and defeated him on the cross. . . . And in order to triumph perfectly, he wished to seize the dwelling of his kingdom and to bind him in his house which is hell. For this reason, he descended thence, devastated his things, and carried off his spoils. . . . Just as Christ had received the power and the possession of heaven and earth, he wished also to receive the possession of hell."[33]

Hell, as well as paradise, is now found *in Christ* insofar as it does not escape his knowledge and sovereignty.

But can this experience of hell, which is traditionally referred to on Holy Saturday, not be theologically grounded already in the reality of the abandonment of Christ on the cross? It would be necessary to consider the cry of Mark 15:34 not only as a momentary sense of dereliction experienced by Jesus shortly before his death but as the theological interpretation of his experience of dying, of his death as a "descent to the netherworld."

I think that the Gospel of Mark permits such a theological openness. There is a *weak point* in the conception of Urs von Balthasar: the absolute passivity of Christ in his descent to the netherworld—his being, so to speak, sin in a pure state.

M.-J. Nicolas has noted this very well: "The extraordinary pages in which von Balthasar develops his thought . . . shed light on the theological significance of the descent to the netherworld as a participation of the 'soul' of Jesus in the state of 'death' which Sheol symbolizes. But is his soul already glorified in this state when he announces salvation to the dead and to all the infernal powers, or does it, on the contrary, continue its passion in its most dramatic and most redemptive aspects? Must one see in the descent to the netherworld the fulfillment itself of the redemptive Mystery, since the abandonment on the cross is insufficient and unable to attain such profundity in the experience of 'Evil'? One hesitates to enter on this second way which does not appear at all in the accounts of the passion, nor in St. Paul, nor in St. John."[34]

In short, the element of *resurrection* is lacking in von Balthasar's descent to the netherworld. It is as risen that Jesus, eternalized in his love of abandonment where he solidarizes with man estranged from God, reaches all men of all times. It is thus necessary to affirm with Fr. X. Durrwell: "In his *glorifying* death, Christ encounters men in their death; in his paschal mystery, he is the eschatological point of salvific encounter and of the gathering of men in their death."[35]

Finally, I should like to draw attention to the fact that the penetration of Jesus into the depths of hell has salvific value not only for the dead but also for the living. The Fathers of the Church do not fail to apply it to the present life: the descent to the netherworld "is repeated every time the Lord penetrates into the depths of the *disperata corda*."[36] The experience of hell, then, must necessarily have some foundation in the *life* of the incarnate Son. One has to situate it in the abandonment as a theological understanding of his death on the cross. In the abandonment by God experienced on the cross, the "descent to the netherworld" can become the glad tidings (cf. 1 Cor 2:2) addressed to the living: God reaches them in the hell of their loneliness, anguish, evil, and absence of God. In his reality of abandonment, Jesus becomes for the living—as he was for the dead—the fixed passageway from the hell of the absence of God to the paradise of communion with God, from darkness to light, from nothingness to plenitude, from death to life.

Notes

1. G. Jouassard, "L'abandon du Christ en croix dans la tradition du IV et V siècles," *Recherche de science religieuse* (1925); P. Foresi, "L'abbandono di Gesù in croce," in *Mariopoli,* (1962), nos. 3–5.

2. "Commentary on Ps 37, 6," in Expositions of the Psalms; cf. also the commentary on Ps 70 (PL 36, 882) and Epistle 140 (PL 33, 543f). Thus also Leo the Great: "Our Lord Jesus Christ, our head, assuming all the members of his body in himself, cried out at his crucifixion with the voice of his redeemed ones, with the words already expressed in the psalm: 'My God, my God, why have you abandoned me?' " (Sermo 16; PL 54, 372). But he also maintains the realism of the abandonment experienced by Jesus himself: "That our Lord was abandoned to the passion was both the will of the Father and his own will, in such a way that the Father not only abandoned him but in a certain way he abandoned himself, not by violent divisions but with a voluntary offer" (Sermo 17; PL 54, 372).

3. Series in Mattheum, 135 (PG 13, 1785–1787).

4. Thus Athanasius: "Whether he wept or was troubled, the Word as such did not weep nor was he troubled, because that belongs to the flesh. If he prayed that the chalice might pass him by, it was not his divinity that experienced anguish but his human nature. The words 'why have you abandoned me?' are understood as if he had really suffered (in his human nature)" (PG 26, 439).

In his work *Why Christ Is One,* directed against Nestorius, Cyril of Alexandria presents this broad vision of the redemption: "When we became accursed through the transgression of Adam, we fell into the snares of death to be abandoned by God. But now in Christ all has become new, and our initial situation has returned. For this reason, it was necessary that the second Adam, having come from Heaven, immune from any sin whatsoever, the most pure and immaculate fruit of our race, i.e., Christ, liberate human nature from its punishment, attract to himself the celestial benevolence of the Father, and make the abandonment cease by means of his obedience and complete submission. In fact, he 'committed no sin,' and human nature attained in him a totally irreprehensible innocence, to the point of now being able to cry freely: 'My God, my God, why have you abandoned me?' Consider in fact that the Only-Begotten utters these words once he had become man, insofar as he had made himself one of us and in the name of all humanity. . . . He implored the benevolence of the Father not for himself but for us."

5. Eusebius also (PG 22, 282). Ambrose: "Jesus cried in a loud voice: 'My God, my God, look at me; why have you abandoned me?' Near death, the man raises a cry because of his separation from the divinity" (PL 15, 1929).

6. Art. cit., in *Mariopoli* (1962), no. 3, p. 8.

7. Cf. P. Foresi, art. cit., in *Mariopoli* (1962), no. 5, p. 18.

8. H. Urs von Balthasar, "Mysterium paschale," in *Mysterium salutis*, III/2:212f, n. 1.

9. Ibid., 156.

10. Ch. Duquoc, *Christologie. Essai dogmatique* (Paris: Cerf, 1972), II:46.

11. Cited by Ch. Duquoc, op. cit., 45. Elsewhere, in the sermon for the 16th Sunday after the Feast of the Holy Trinity, Tauler expresses himself thus: "When he was the most abandoned by men, he was the most pleasing to his Father, when he cried 'God, God, my God, how you have abandoned me!' " (*Opere,* Paoline, ed. [Alba, 1976], 506). As one can see, for these mystics, the abandonment is a subjective experience. It is situated on the psychological level and does not imply a real rejection on the part of God.

12. The abandonment of Christ as a model for Christian life is a theme that is found under different aspects throughout the centuries.

In the mystics just considered, the abandonment of Jesus is seen as a model of detachment from the world, from all that could be an obstacle to the ever more perfect union with the divinity.

In these centuries and in the following ones, Jesus always becomes the model for dying believers, inundated by the fear of death: "Jesus Christ, the Holy One of God . . . did he not die in this state of desolation?" (the priest Boileau of the seventeenth century) (cf. J. Delumeau, *Le péché et la peur,* [Paris: Fayard, 1983], 361).

In the last century, S. Kierkegaard sees the abandonment of Jesus as a model in the trial of despair:

" 'My God, my God, why have you abandoned me?' These words are a consolation for the imitators (of Christ). Why were so many martyrs at the height of their sufferings and in a moment of weakness not within a hair's breadth of losing the idea of themselves (= of despairing), as if they were abandoned by God? . . . It is for this reason that the Model consoles with those words, showing that that trial is indispensable. In a certain sense, one may well say that being abandoned by God is indispensable in order completely to exhaust the human before God. . . . But, if that is indispensable, then there is nothing depressing in the thought of having to remember that one also bore this human suffering of feeling abandoned by God . . . " (*Diario 1854,* Brescia, 1963, II:528f). The thought of Kierkegaard comes close to that of the mystics. In our century, finally, I shall cite the case of D. Bonhoeffer. For him, the imitation of the abandoned Jesus is an aspect of "carrying the cross" to follow Christ and thus to carry out the work of salvation. For Bonhoeffer, the abandonment of Christ which it is a question of sharing does not consist in bearing sufferings in general but in the specific aspect of suffering endured because of Christ: the aspect of *rejection,* of scorn, of the abandonment inherent in such suffering. "Certainly," the author writes, "only the suffering proper to Christ is a conciliatory suffering. But because Christ suffered on account of the sins of the world, because all the weight of guilt fell on him, and because Jesus Christ imputed the fruits of his suffering to those who follow him, temptation and sin also fall upon his disciple, cover him with opprobrium, and chase him like the scapegoat outside the gates of the city, so that the Christian becomes a bearer of sins and of guilt for other men. . . . In the strength of the suffering of Christ, it is possible for him to triumph over the sins that fall upon him in the measure that he forgives them. Whoever refuses to take up his cross, whoever does not wish to give his life to suffering and rejection on the part of men, loses communion with Christ; he is not obedient" (*Le prix de la grâce,* ed. Delachaux et Niestlé [Neuchâtel, 1962], 56). This is profound reflection in which the believer becomes "sin" like Christ and as such experiences the abandonment of God felt in being rejected by men. Unfortunately, it is seen in a juridical conception of the redemption: Christ undergoes the *punishment* for our sins (cf. p. 181).

13. "The Third Sermon on the Exaltation of the Cross" (*Opere spirituali,* ed. Paoline [Alba, 1971], 595).

Suso does not fail to fall into the rather widespread dolorism of the time: the abandonment is part of the material describing the pains of Jesus by which the people liked to be moved. In the *Booklet of Eternal Wisdom,* he has Jesus say: "Listen! While I stood there, so completely deprived of help and abandoned, with oozing wounds, with my eyes full of tears, my arms extended, and the veins of all my members stretched in mortal agony, I raised my sorrowful voice and cried out piously to my Father, saying: 'My God, my God, how you have abandoned me!' And yet, my will was united to his according to the eternal disposition . . . " (*Opere spirituali,* 315).

14. *Opere,* Postulazione Generale dei Carmelitani Scalzi, Rome, 1967, pp. 92f.

15. B. Carra de Vaux Saint-Cyr, *L'abandon du Christ en croix,* Problèmes actuels de Christologie, ed. M. Bouësse and J.-J. Latour (Paris: Desclée de Brouwer, 1965), 305. This is taken up by Duquoc in *Christologie,* cit., 41.

16. Op. cit., III/2:157.

17. *L'institution chrètienne,* (Geneva: Labor et fides, 1955), II:209f. Cited by Duquoc, op. cit., 47 and 63.

18. Thus K. Barth in *Dogmatik im Grundriβ,* (Zurich: EVZ-Verlag, 1947), 119–126; 134–138; or again, D. Bonhoeffer, in *Ethique* (Geneva: Labor et fides, 1949), 48. Urs von Balthasar has also been influenced by this.

19. Op. cit., 48f; for the text of Bossuet, p. 50.

20. *La croix de Jésus* (Paris: Cerf, 1937), 155–156.

21. Op cit., 50f. The way Duquoc himself conceives the abandonment of Christ is expressed on p. 40. He distinguishes three stages of dereliction: "The failure of a task, the distress of the just man, and the estrangement from God or his abandonment. The third moment is to be understood in relation with the other two." These are existential factors which can, in fact, explain the psychological experience of abandonment. But what is its theological value?

22. Cf. the impressive documentation gathered by Jean Delumeau, *Le péché et la peur. La culpabilisation en occident XIII–XVIII siècles,* (Paris: Fayard, 1983); for our theme, cf. esp. pp. 321–331; 467–469.

23. Op. cit., 331.

24. From a meditation by L. Tronson, *Retraite ecclésiastique suivie de méditations,* cited by Delumeau, in op. cit., 328.

25. J. Moltmann, "Kreuzestheologie heute," in idem, *Zukunft der Schöpfung. Gesammelte Aufsätze* (Munich, 1977), 80f.

26. Xavier Léon-Dufour, op. cit., 151.

27. Moltmann, op. cit., 287.

28. H. Urs von Balthasar, *Herrlichkeit* (Einsiedeln, 1980), III:213.

29. H. Urs von Balthasar develops his conception in "Mysterium paschale," in *Mysterium Salutis,* III/2:243–255; he takes it up in a more synthetic way in *Herrlichkeit,* III/2:211–217.

30. *Jésus devant sa vie et sa mort* (Paris: Aubier, 1971), 240, n. 30.

31. *L'au-delà retrouvé* (Paris: Desclée, 1975), 96, n. 26.

32. "Symbolum apostolorum expositio," in Opuscula theologica II, no. 926.

33. Ibid., 928.

34. *Théologie de la résurrection* (Paris: Desclée, 1982), 33, n. 13.

35. *La résurrection de Jésus mystère de salut,* 10th ed. (Paris: Cerf, 1976), 152, n. 46.

36. Gregory the Great, cited by Urs von Balthasar, "Mysterium paschale," p. 249. A similar application is made in Thomas, op. cit., n. 930.

CHAPTER 6

Present Interpretations of the Cry of Abandonment

Let us now take into consideration the way exegetes today understand the cry of abandonment uttered by Jesus on the cross.

A Cry of Despair?

At times, the cry of abandonment has been understood by some exegetes of a rationalist tendency—thus by deniers of the divinity of Christ—as the cry of a desperate man, the cry of a man who has totally missed his existence and sees his messianic claims crumble inexorably before him.

This thesis does violence to the profound meaning that underlies the text itself. From the preceding analysis it has become clear that the account has been constructed in such a way as to insert the passion of Jesus into the great Old Testament tradition of the suffering servant, which is an authentic interpretation of that which Jesus really lived. And every reader knew that in the perspective of the suffering servant his cry of lament would not be lost in the void; rather, he could count on a liberating intervention of Yahweh.

There is in fact no psalm of lamentation or song of the suffering servant that ends in despair. In particular, Psalm 22 concludes with a proclamation of trust in Yahweh:

> For he has not spurned nor disdained
> the wretched man in his misery,
> Nor did he turn his face away from him,

but when he cried out to him, he heard him. . . .
And to him my soul shall live;
   my descendants shall serve him . . . (Ps 22:25, 31).

The cry of abandonment, then, remains essentially a *prayer*—
the desperate man no longer implores—and thus a testimony of
faithfulness to him who is experienced as Absent, a faith that
is exalted in the Mystery of that God who is near yet hides himself.

Let us not forget the key that Mark gives us in the words of
Jesus in the garden of Gethsemani:

"*Abba* . . . let it be as you would have it, not as I" (Mk 14:36).
The abandonment is understood correctly only in the light of
these words.

It is necessary, moreover, to be attentive to the theological
value of the term that introduces Psalm 22:2 in Mark 15:34: "Jesus *cried* in a loud voice." The expression not only has a descrip-
tive or realistic value but in its biblical meaning indicates precisely
the cry of pain addressed to Yahweh by the just man who is oppressed and persecuted: the *cry* is a form of prayer that arises in
a situation of extreme necessity.

Stauffer writes: "The 'cry' of man is not a useless cry that gets
lost in the deaf and insensitive void but the call to an interlocutor
who listens to us. The man who places all his trust in himself 'is
stricken dumb in his pain.' The man, on the other hand, who
knows himself to stand before a divine interlocutor can open himself to him in his torment, whereas he who is ignorant of this
openness and this prayer is swallowed in his loneliness. Even the
biblical man knows the desolation of the one who feels abandoned by God. But from the depths of this desperate and deadly
loneliness there gushes forth the cry that expresses total submission to the God who stands before him. . . . 'Out of the depths I
cry to you, O Lord' (Ps 130:1)."[1]

These indications suffice to discard the thesis of despair.

A Cry of Trust?

There does exist an opposite interpretation, especially on Catholic terrain: from the depths of his suffering, Jesus proclaims his unshakable trust in God. It is this trust of Christ who abandons himself to the Father that lends the text its tone: there is no place for a real experience of dereliction. "Psalm 22, from which these words are drawn, is not a psalm of despair but of trust: it is therefore not a question of a real abandonment," according to José Alonso Diaz' commentary on Mark 15:34.[2]

This interpretation—in obvious reaction to those who consider the cry of Jesus as that of a desperate man—has different elements in its favor. The account of the crucifixion with its various references and allusions to verses of Psalm 22 already suggests that the evangelist has the entire psalm in mind and not only a specific verse.

The history of Israel before and after Christ knows of pious Jews persecuted for their convictions who died with a prayer, a psalm on their lips. Jesus would have inserted himself into this current of testimony: "It is probable that Jesus recited in a low voice the entire psalm in which the sufferings of his passion were prefigured, with the exception of the first words which he cried out in order to emphasize that in this instant he was living precisely the situation represented in it. In spite of its literal formulation, his lament was in no way a gesture of despair. On the contrary, it was an act of total abandonment into the hands of the Father, so much so that he cried out a second time, saying " 'Father, into your hands I commend my spirit' (Lk 23:46)."[3]

I do not wish to enter into the merits of this too historicizing and harmonizing interpretation. I shall dwell on the idea that Jesus on the cross recited the entire Psalm 22 which, in effect, is not on the whole a lament or a cry of despair but the prayer of one who trusts in God and expects with certainty a salvific intervention from him.

Moreover, the literary usage of writing only the first words of a prayer while having, however, its whole content in mind was also in existence. In the Church also, there is the custom of des-

ignating the entire prayer with the initial words: the "Our Father," the "Ave Maria," the "Magnificat," etc. The evangelist
would thus have transcribed only the first verse of Psalm 22, leaving the completion to the reader!

> In the Jewish tradition up until today the books of the Penta-
> teuch, its weekly divisions, and various prayers are cited with
> the first words or with the main sentence. Even some psalms are
> still cited in this way, for example, *Ashrei* (Ps 1) or *Al naharot
> Bavel* (Ps 137). It is probable that at the time of the first Gospels
> Psalm 22 was also cited according to this usage by the first main
> sentence. In other words, the Gospel tells that at the point of
> death Jesus recited Psalm 22. If this is the case, there are no
> problems to be solved. As we have seen, the psalm begins in de-
> spair but ends in the enthusiasm of faith and of hope. . . . How
> can we explain the fact that the majority of Christian theolo-
> gians have accepted the idea that Jesus died uttering words of
> despair and did not realize that he died reciting Psalm 22? Per-
> haps the reason is simply that Christian scholars did not think
> of this limited and negligible Jewish usage of citing a book or a
> chapter by its first sentence.[4]

In spite of the seriousness of the arguments mentioned above
in favor of the idea that the evangelist only cited the first verse of
Psalm 22 by way of introduction, which psalm Jesus would then
have recited in its entirety in order to proclaim his trust in God,
this hypothesis does not hold when one is attentive to the Gospel
text.

It is not to be doubted that Mark (and Matthew) presents the
passion as the entrance of Jesus into an ever greater loneliness,
having been repudiated by the crowd, by the disciples, and by the
religious authorities. In line with this orientation of the passion,
the reader can discern nothing other in the sole articulate cry of
the Crucified than the culminating point of his loneliness: the passion leads Jesus to abandonment even on the part of God.

This general observation is confirmed by various indications:
Mark introduces the verse with "Jesus cried in a loud voice,"

which necessarily attracts attention to the content of the verse cited and not to the entire psalm.

He then transcribes the text in Aramaic and thus not in Hebrew, the official language of the psalms, but in Jesus' mother tongue. That excludes Mark's having had the entire psalm in mind. Moreover, as is the case with other words of Jesus related in his Gospel—"Talitha kum" (Mk 5:41), for example—the evangelist adds the translation.[5]

All this shows that Mark considers the cry as a true and proper "*utterance of Jesus*" and not as the recitation of a psalm. If Mark had wanted to remind the reader of a text of the Old Testament, he would have added: "for Scripture has it" (see Mk 14:27). Finally, let us recall that already in the pre-Markan tradition the account of the crucifixion is presented against the background of the *passio justi,* thus as it was understood in Judaism. We are in the line of a theology of martyrdom where there is no longer a question of an experience of abandonment.

In light of this interpretation of the "suffering servant," the cry of Psalm 22 appears then as an unexpected, extraneous element (cf. Chapter 3). Two consequences follow:

• It is precisely this unexpected character of Psalm 22:2 in the context of the *passio justi* that invites the reader to give all its value to the content of this verse, to its immediate sense of abandonment by God.

• But it is the very same context of the *passio justi* that must also orient the interpretation of the cry of abandonment. And although one respects its proper content, one should not make it the cry of a desperate man or a simple formula of introduction for a psalm of praise.

Let us not forget in fact that in spite of all the seriousness of this cry it was interpreted by the community as the cry of a just man martyred on account of his justice; and it saw in the suffering itself the proof of his election by God. It is *this* context that should illuminate v. 2 of Psalm 22 (in Mk 15:34 in the primitive tradition) rather than the (optimistic) continuation of this psalm.[6]

The conclusion appears obvious enough: in the intention of the evangelist it is necessary to take as seriously as possible the state of abandonment that is expressed by the content of the cry of the Crucified.

A great number of exegetes and theologians today are tending in this direction. By way of example, I shall relate what J. Galot has written:

Undoubtedly, the invocation was intentionally taken up with the purpose of expressing the apparent absence of the Father on Calvary. By "abandoning" Jesus to death, the Father seems to veil his face as Father. The term "Eli" not only demonstrates the fulfillment of a prophetic text but assumes a new value in the context of the filial relationship of Jesus to the Father. It evokes the drama of the Son who no longer succeeds in recognizing the face of the Father in his suffering. . . . Jesus no longer felt the paternal presence.

The abandonment is felt more deeply by Jesus since his filial contact with the Father was strong. How is one to characterize such an abandonment? From the biblical point of view, there is above all an objective abandonment that consists in the fact that Jesus is abandoned to death and that the Father does not intervene to save his life. . . . Moreover, this abandonment seems to imply in Jesus a disavowal on the part of the Father. He had given a message to humanity, guaranteeing its authenticity with the authority of the Father. Now, in the moment in which he gives his life in sacrifice to testify to the truth of his preaching, he seems to await a solemn approbation from the Father in vain. This is so much so that Saul will very soon base his zeal as a persecutor of Christians on the fact of the death of Jesus interpreted as a demonstration of divine disavowal. . . .

Furthermore, the abandonment bears a subjective aspect. Jesus "feels" abandoned; he experiences affectively the void of an absence. From this point of view, one understands even more easily that the suffering is essentially a filial suffering. The Son is anguished in his human feelings because he has lost the joy of the presence of the Father, and especially in circumstances in which he would have valued such support. Even though it cuts

deeply into his human nature, the intensity of the anguish de-
rives from his personality as Son.

The interrogative "why?" is no less characteristic of this filial
suffering. Jesus poses the problem that many have posed before
him and that very many will pose after him. Besides the concrete
fact of sensible pain, there is the torment for the human mind
of not understanding its meaning. Feeling abandoned by the Father, Jesus is disconcerted by the paternal attitude of which he
had experienced so many comforting manifestations and which
seems so different in this critical hour. The abandonment posed
an insoluble problem for him, a problem common to all who
are afflicted by great trials but which assumes an exceptional
value in Jesus given that fact that the "why" is addressed by the
Son to the Father. Even for the Son, suffering is a mystery, the
depths of which human intelligence is unable to sound.⁻

The Proper Meaning of the Cry of Abandonment

One cannot but share the principal points placed in the limelight
by J. Galot:

• The content of Psalm 22:2 must be taken literally: it is a question of precisely an experience of abandonment by God.

• The abandonment must be understood on the basis of the
being and the mission of the incarnate Son. One cannot therefore
reduce the situation of the Crucified to that of the psalmist. In this
sense, the author makes his an observation of J. Moltmann: "It
is not correct to interpret the cry of Jesus in the sense of Psalm
22; rather, it is more correct here to interpret the words of the
psalm in the sense of the situation of Jesus."[8]

It is true that Galot places himself in the perspective of his
book, the original title of which, *Dieu souffre-t-il?* (Does God
Suffer?), clearly formulates his purpose. His analysis is consequently based on the psychological experience of abandonment
had by Jesus on the cross. The author cannot therefore place the

historical authenticity of the articulate cry in doubt for any reason.

All the considerations that Galot expounds in the above-cited text serve to underscore the greatness and originality of Jesus' torment. The investigation of J. Galot is perfectly legitimate, but in the intention guiding my work, one would only go halfway were one to stop at these data. The aim of this study is in fact not simply to understand the greatness of the suffering of Jesus, the Son, manifested in his cry. It is a question of interpreting the cry in its revelational reality and in its salvific value for man.

I should like to delineate more clearly in what sense the interpretation of Mark 15:24 should be carried out.

A first point: the cry of abandonment must be understood and interpreted from its own context, i.e., from the account of Mark and Matthew, without introducing an utterance of Jesus from another Gospel and thus from another theological view in order to attenuate its crudeness, with the risk of altering its theological meaning. Concretely, one should not bring in the last utterance of Jesus in the Gospel of Luke: "Father, into your hands I commend my spirit" (Lk 23:46).

In fact, in the Gospel of Mark, the cry of abandonment, the only utterance of Jesus on the cross, is placed into relation with the death of Jesus and is its theological interpretation.

The abandonment indicates that Christ faced death in the greatest torment, which—according to the typically biblical meaning—consists not only in the integral loss of life (body and soul) but also in the loss of God. It is a truth to be understood essentially in its theological and not psychological value (even if such an experience of the Crucified is not to be excluded).

Certainly, the reader of the Gospel knows that it is not a question of a cry of despair true and proper nor of a cry of rebellion: the dereliction is experienced in the extreme obedience of the "suffering servant" *par excellence*. His trust in the divine presence precisely in the experience of his absence is implicit in this cry which brings to a close a whole spiritual tradition of Israel but above all a unique filial relationship.

To appeal to the last utterance of Jesus in the Gospel of Luke which belongs to another, equally valid, theological context in order to grant the Crucified a happy ending appears then all the more inappropriate because it contradicts what Mark—and the tradition before him—wants to have understood: the cry of abandonment interprets precisely *the death* of Jesus and does not consist in a passing experience that was resolved before his death.

The divine intervention does not in fact consist in some consolation intended to brighten the last instants of Christ's life. The response of God takes place precisely in death and is thus a victory over death with all that death entails: estrangement from God and loss of life. It consists in a creative act, the resurrection. For this reason, in the understanding of some Fathers of the Church, the final loud cry (Mk 15:37) is understood as the birth cry of the new creation.

A second point: if this is the case, on what reality can the meaning of the cry of abandonment rest?

On the historical fact that Jesus actually uttered the first verse of Psalm 22 on the cross? We saw in Chapter 2 that it is not practically possible by means of historical criticism to pronounce oneself for or against the historicity of the articulate cry. In favor of the latter, one must point to the unexpected presence of the latter in the context of a theology of martyrdom (but see Chapter 3 also, section 2). The cry of Jesus may therefore be found at the origin of the importance that Psalm 22 assumes from the beginning of the tradition in the account of the crucifixion. In favor of its historicity, one can also note the formulation in Aramaic and not in Hebrew of the psalm verse.

But the fact that we are unable to prove the historicity of the cry does not in any way invalidate the faith or the legitimacy of theological reflection on this Gospel text.

Is it then possible to point to the fact that Jesus at least had the *experience* of abandonment, even if *ex hypothesi* he did not explicitly cry out Psalm 22:2?

It is certainly very probable that Jesus experienced such an abandonment. But what means do we have of knowing the psyche of Jesus at that moment? Can we found a theological interpretation on a psychological datum alone, on the subjective experience of dereliction had by Jesus on the cross? How could we demonstrate it? And what if on the cross Jesus spent the last few moments of his earthly existence in a serene relationship with the Father, as the Gospel of Luke, for example, describes it?

In reality, the incontestable historical fact on which the theological interpretation of the cry of abandonment rests is Jesus' *death on the cross*. In the context of the "suffering servant" and even more of the filial reality of Jesus, Psalm 22:2 interprets the death of Jesus as a death *on the cross*, knowing that the cross was considered at that time and in Judaism as the wood of the curse.[9]

It is precisely along these lines that the theological thought of Paul on the crucified Jesus is situated (cf. Gal 3:13, and what he deduces from it in 1 Corinthians 1:17ff, for example). The rest remains within the field of the possible and of the probable but cannot be demonstrated: that is due in particular to the nature of the Gospel text which nonetheless merits our trust (cf. the Preface).

In saying this I have absolutely no intention of denying the historicity of the articulate cry or the experience of dereliction had on the cross. I am simply saying that they cannot be demonstrated with the methods of the historical sciences. The Gospel account is not a chronicle of facts. This also obliges us to overcome a kind of reflection that remains on the psychological level.

It is sure that we are in the presence of an authentic interpretation by faith of the meaning of the death of Christ, thus one like that of Luke or John. From this point of view, Duquoc is correct in writing: "The aims pursued by the four evangelists are not identical, even if all have only one desire: to testify that Jesus is the Son of the living God, the Savior of the world. They therefore organize their material in dependence on their own theology. It would be an error to want to harmonize the accounts. It would also be a mistake to privilege the point of view of one or two evangelists in an absolute way. The theology of the abandonment of Christ on the cross will thus be unable to omit the Lukan perspective in which the hope of Jesus in God, his Father, is placed in relief" (op. cit., 44).

A third point: Jesus exposes his state of abandonment with the help of Psalm 22. Now, among the psalms of lamentation, Psalm 22 occupies a quite particular place.[10] In general, the pray-er, who is in a condition of extreme difficulty and danger, implores Yahweh and prays that God not abandon him:

> Hide not your face from me;
>> do not in anger repel your servant.
> You are my helper: cast me not off;
>> forsake me not, O God my savior (Ps 27:9).

In Psalm 22, on the other hand, the situation is quite different: the psalmist is already experiencing the abandonment, and yet he turns to God experienced as absent. It is no longer only a trust in divine assistance but a faith that penetrates into the night of God.

This second point orients us in focusing on what is central in the trial of the abandoned Jesus. In biblical language, being abandoned means that God has not come to one's assistance, that he does not intervene in order to save man from the dangers of sickness or from his enemies. The trust of the prayer, which comes to light at the end of the psalm of lamentation, is then translated as the certainty of divine help and not infrequently acquires the flavor of vengeance on one's adversaries.

For Jesus, the abandonment takes on an entirely different sense: it is no longer the entreaty of a divine intervention on his behalf, the request for a help that will liberate him from his adversaries,[11] or that demonstrates his innocence to his executioners. In obedience to the Father, Jesus had already accepted drinking the chalice to the dregs. "This cry is no longer a crying for help or of vengeance, it is the *cry for God himself*" (Stauffer). Jesus is in search of his God; it is the night of faith of the incarnate Son.

The characteristic content of the abandonment of Jesus is thus the suffering of the "loss of God," of his absence or estrangement: this is the "torment in his torments."[12] Its newness with respect to the agony in the garden of Gethsemani lies in the theological value his pain assumes.

In the abandonment, Jesus attains human suffering and

death—and, more generally, the existential situation of man—
and makes them his own in the more painful and profound reality
of the "loss of God."

Every true pain in its essential "why?" poses the problem of
God. "The man who suffers in excess always believes himself to
be abandoned by God. This God shows himself to him as mysterious and unintelligible; he shatters the happiness that he himself had bestowed. Whoever cries to God in such suffering is at
bottom in unison with the death cry of the dying Christ, the Son
of God."[13]

The denudation of God in the incarnation (cf. Phil 2:6ff) thus
attains its fullness in the abandonment of Christ who identifies
himself with human suffering and experiences the loss of God in
its most disconcerting reality.

In the abandonment, Jesus lives to an extreme the nearness of
God to man in his extreme solidarity with humanity.

Notes

1. *Grande lessico del Nuovo Testamento* (Brescia: Paideia, 1966),
II:298.

2. *Vangelo secondo Marco,* Nuovo Testamento, ed. Juan Leal
(Rome: Città Nuova, 1970), in loco.

3. S. Del Paramos, *Vangelo secondo Matteo,* Nuovo Testamento
(Rome: Città Nuova, 1970), 413.

4. E. Fromm, *Voi sarete come dèi* (Rome, 1970), 155f.

5. Cf. X. Léon-Dufour, op. cit., 153–154.

6. I shall mention another interpretation that is today obsolete even
if it was common in the not too distant past. It erroneously understood
the way Jesus fulfilled the Scriptures, a misunderstanding perhaps owing
to an unskilled reading of certain formulas of introduction in the Gospel
for Old Testament citations of the type: Jesus did such and such "in order that what had been said by the prophets might be fulfilled" (the so-
called *Reflexionszitaten* of Matthew; or John 19:28).

The Old Testament was seen as a book containing precise predictions
concerning the Messiah and his operations which Jesus realized as soon
as the occasion presented itself in his life. Here is an example taken from

a meditation of Charles de Foucauld. He has Jesus say: "These words (i.e., the cry of abandonment), my son, are words of obedience. I suffer thus in order to obey the ideal that God has made for himself of the Messiah, the conception of the Messiah that was in the divine mind before the creation of my human soul, which God described in the prophecies, which he revealed to me from the first moment of the creation of my soul, and to which I submitted myself immediately with all my heart. . . . Hung on a cross out of obedience, out of conformity to the divine will . . . I manifest my obedience to him, the conformity of my heart and works to his divine will, by citing the first verses of a prediction that I voluntarily fulfill in the same instant. . . . It is as if I were to say: 'Behold, Father, I fulfill what you have foretold of me. Behold me present on the cross, before your prophecy, to conform myself to it. Behold your command which I cite; and behold its execution in me' " (*Opere spirituali*, ed. Paoline, [Rome, 1983], 261).

In this interpretation, the content of the cry is indifferent: neither despair nor song of trust but obedient recitation, a way for Jesus to remain in his role of Messiah.

7. *Il mistero della sofferenza di Dio* (Assisi: Cittadella ed., 1975), 47–51.

8. Jean Galot, *Dieu souffre-t-il?* (Paris: Lethielleux, 1976), 52–55.

9. Of course, this whole discourse presupposes the Jewish context of the condemnation of Jesus, i.e., he was condemned within Jewish legislation for religious motives (even if the official pretext and the material execution were the work of the Romans). In fact, during the Jewish War (66–70 A.D.), for example, many Jews were condemned to the cross by the *Romans*, i.e., by the enemy, and they were not considered by their co-religionists as accursed but precisely as martyrs.

10. Cf. J. Gnilka, *Das Evangelium nach Markus*, II:322, n. 77. The observation of Gnilka seems correct to me, even if I should not exaggerate the author's affirmation of the originality of Psalm 22 with respect to the other psalms of lamentation. Certainly, turning to God in the moment in which one experiences his absence corresponds to a quite different situation from that in which one invokes God so that he may not abandon one. But, as I have said, I should not exaggerate the originality of Psalm 22. Other psalms, in fact—not cited by the author, like Psalms 13:2; 42:10; 88:15—reflect a situation similar to that of Psalm 22. Moreover, Psalm 22 possesses as a whole the same schema that we find in the other psalms of this type: lamentation, proclamation of trust, prayer for help; song of praise and of thanksgiving.

It is in the mouth of Jesus—and thus in the reinterpretation of Psalm 22 in the light of the passion on the part of the tradition—that the beginning of the psalm acquires all its originality. Understood as an "utterance of Jesus" (and that draws attention to the content of the verse itself) and in Jesus' line of behavior during his passion (see the prayer in Gethsemani and his silence afterward), Psalm 22 is no longer seen as an invocation of help in a situation of abandonment but as letting oneself be borne by God in the abandonment and thus as an experience that directly regards the personal relationship of Jesus with his God.

11. This could be the characteristic of the prayer in the garden of Gethsemani: "(O Father), you have the power to do all things. Take this cup away from me." But there is already a willingness to accept a qualitatively different situation that goes beyond the prayer of the psalmist: "But let it be as you would have it, not as I" (Mk 14:36).

In his last book, P. Grelot writes: "The fact that God abandons Jesus to death constitutes only one aspect of the experience of the cross. Now, at Gethsemani, the acceptance of the 'cup of death' in order to fulfill the will of the Father already bears a consent to this abandonment. Now, it is within the man, Jesus, in whom the person of the Son was 'made flesh' without confusion, that the relationship to God is felt as a kind of absence. . . . On the cross, the faith of Jesus lies in the heart of the night" (*Dans les angoisses l'espérance. Enquête biblique* [Paris: Ed. du Seuil, 1983], 228).

12. J. Moltmann, op. cit., 142.

13. Cf. ibid., 263–267.

CHAPTER 7

The Abandonment of Christ: Revelation of the Salvific Love of God

The Abandonment of Jesus and the Human Condition of Sin

The abandonment of Christ on the cross presents itself as the response of God to the scandal of man's suffering, of the death of the innocent, of anxiety, and of all the "why's" that have no answer.[1] It is the definitive "yes" of God to fallen man, to man estranged from God. It is a "yes" that does not remove this suffering, does not explain it, and does not justify it, but inserts it into the trinitarian Mystery of God, into the Father-Son relationship of love experienced and revealed on the cross. Now, every cry of abandonment involves the Trinity, every "why?" belongs to the very Mystery of divinity.

A first aspect that the reality of the abandonment brings to light is the solidarity with the human condition experienced to the depths. It is in the abandonment that Christ—and God—attains the maximum of "poverty" characteristic of the "self-denudation" of the Incarnation (cf. 2 Cor 8:9).

The salvific dimension of this solidarity has been noted by different theologians: "The Crucified has become the brother of the despised, abandoned, and oppressed."[2] And Martelet writes: "Christ has sunk the shaft of his cross so deep into the sea, with it he has explored the unfathomable depths of the human ocean to such an extent that there exists no pain, no darkness, no loneliness, no contempt of others or of oneself, no horror, no aban-

115

donment, no cry, nothing except hell itself which is the absurd negation of this salvific love, nothing at all that is not found in him who has not refused anything of the misery he finds in us."[3]

It is the situation of human sin that—theologically speaking—best mirrors the abandonment of Jesus suffered as the loss of God. The human condition is not in fact characterized only by limits—and consequent negativity, suffering, and existential anxiety—owing to man's creaturehood but also by that other mystery which sin is, the evil by which man destroys himself and fails in his vocation as man, in his individual and social dimension: the situation *par excellence* of separation from God.

Jesus has descended into this existential failure also and reaches man in the prison of his sin.

> Jesus, with all his love, experiences the rupture that exists between the sinner and God as an excruciating absence, as a flawless loneliness. . . . It is the Father who with all his love sustains the exhausted Son, leads him into the ultimate depths of the abandonment, makes him penetrate into the loneliness of sinners to the point of dying their death.[4]

It is fidelity to the Father and not rebellion that carries Christ far from God, far also from the felt experience and the support of love, even if precisely this love is the exegesis of the event: the extreme abandonment manifests the extreme communion of the Son with the Father.

Therefore, the abandonment does not close Jesus in the prison of sin, but, paradoxically, expresses his perfect unity with God. And that provokes the radical change of sign, the decisive turning point for the human condition. Evil has been vanquished on its own terrain, death can become the material of Life, and estrangement from God encounter with him.

> Christ could experience death in itself only as such an abandonment by God. Embraced by the obedient yes of the Son, and without losing its terribleness as abandonment by God, death is now transformed into something totally different: the advent of

God in the midst of this empty abandonment and the manifestation of the obedient surrender of the whole man to the holy God in the midst of his apparent perdition and estrangement. This is precisely the wonder of the death of Christ.[5]

In the abandonment experienced by the incarnate Word, God explores the depths of human misery and penetrates into that negativity which is the absence of God. Consequently, in whatever situation he may find himself, man can directly encounter the salvific love of God. In the abandonment on the cross, the presence of the Father characterized itself as absence, silence, and non-intervention so that man in his estrangement from God might experience the nearness of God. If this is the case, sin, negativity, evil, and failure of any kind are denied the last word. "Fallen man is surrounded by the love of God," writes Schoonenberg.[6] The same author expresses these beautiful thoughts:

He who accepts his own failure before God opens a passage way for God to others and to one's own deepest self.

He thereby enters into the deepest mystery of God. God is not a miraculous substitute for what is lacking, not a stopgap. . . . Nor is God the one who arbitrarily distributes success and failure, happiness and pain, life and death among men, as if he were organizing a spectacle for himself. . . . He who confesses Jesus in the garden of olives and on the cross as the Only-Begotten of God knows that God is not insensitive to our death, to our pain, to our failure, and to our anguish. In his Son, he takes them upon himself. And if the Father abandons his Son to this lot, he certainly does not do so as one who commands it from his heavenly throne, nor even less as one who struggles with him, but rather as one who is present in him.

"The Father is with me," "the Father is in me" (Jn 16:32; 10:38; 14:11). The God who in the burning bush united himself to his people with his "I am" (Ex 3:14) now pronounces this same 'I am' in the Son of man elevated on the cross (Jn 8:28).

In spite of the distinction of persons, in virtue of which we must reject patripassionism, *patricompassionism* remains an

implication of our confession: "God is love." He is with us and
in us in our pain, our anguish, our failure.[7]

I should like to place another aspect into relief: the respect that
God in his search for the man estranged from him shows for this
very man.

J. Guillet has noted this: "(Jesus) saves us in his loneliness. . . .
Rejected by all, lost in an entirely hostile world, one against him
to the point of causing his death, Jesus Christ finds in his love the
strength to remain united to us; he finds in his loneliness the point
where he is able to reach us, and to reach us just as we are, just
as he sees us, closed in our refusal, locked up in our hostility. It
is there in fact that he must reach us so that the redemption may
be not the gesture of commiseration of a God touched by our mis-
fortune, but the gesture of justice of a God who does not refrain
from obtaining from his creature the 'yes' for which he created it,
the adhesion in faith that will save it from its loneliness. This is
why Jesus let himself be locked up with us in our hell, this is why
he came alone and defenseless to face our violent deeds, our lies,
and our refusals, to change them at their root, to take us where
we are in our sin, and to turn us back to the Father."[8]

God not only does not impose his plan of salvation on man, he
also counts on human freedom in the growth that will draw man
close to him. He shows this way of acting in the dying Jesus also:
it is, in fact, the *man* Jesus who suffers the abandonment on the
cross and transforms such loneliness into a total expression of
love.

In whatever situation of estrangement from God he may be,
every man can now recognize the face of the crucified Christ, be
"configured" to him, and receive the possibility and the strength
to follow him, to make the experience of Jesus his own, i.e., to
participate actively in his own salvation, in his self-realization, in
his own "divinization."

In communicating his Life and his Love, God respects man as
a being endowed with understanding and will, as a being free and
responsible for himself. Certainly, it is not a question of doing
"works" in the Pauline sense of the term but of accepting one's

own condition of sin every day, of transforming into love, i.e., into the creative action of God, all in man that is estranged from God. In this active passivity, man is more present to himself than ever, co-creator of his new birth, even if everything comes from God.

One reality that comes to fulfillment in the abandonment of Jesus is his function as Mediator.

Certainly, one must not dwell solely on the static side of mediation, i.e., on the fact that in Christ humanity and divinity are ineffably united. The mediatorship is not exhausted in the ontological status of the God-man given at the moment of the Incarnation, even if such a reality is indispensable.

Jesus, the Son, is Mediator in his *humanity* (cf. 1 Tim 2:5); it is a lived mediation, carried forth in his existence.

The mediation of Christ, seen in its dynamic aspect, is oriented toward the climax of his earthly existence: the paschal event which includes death and resurrection.

On the cross, particularly in the abandonment, Jesus is fully Mediator in act for all times. Mark had already made this clear by closely connecting the episode of the torn veil of the temple with the death: in that act on which the cry of abandonment is a commentary, Jesus is the tear between heaven and earth, the place where God and man are joined. At that moment, "Jesus is fully on the side of God and at the same time completely on the side of man: radically solidary with God . . . on the other hand, fully solidary with man."[9] It is in this situation that he opened himself totally to the transforming action of God. The divine action is performed in the most profound and universal solidarity with the human condition that Christ experienced. Jesus is exalted in the presence of God at the moment in which as pure love he consents to penetrating to the depths of the situation of the man estranged from God. It is therefore precisely in this solidarity with the world of sinners, experienced in abandonment, that separation with God is removed, since at that moment Jesus is the most total openness to the God who "restores the dead to life and calls into being those things which had not been" (Rom 4:17).

The Abandoned One, the God of Our Times

Jesus in his abandonment is the God of those without God. He presents himself in a special way as the response to contemporary atheism. This relationship between the abandoned Jesus and atheism has been deeply perceived by J. Moltmann who dedicates many pages of his book *Der gekreuzigte Gott* to this phenomenon of our times.[10]

"What Jesus had presented in the Sermon on the Mount as love of one's enemies was translated . . . in the death of Jesus on the cross into a love that includes those who are without God and without love" (p. 289).

According to the author, Christian theology will have to understand the abandoned Jesus, even identify itself with his cry, if it does not wish to fail before the problematic of the atheism of protest of an Ivan Karamazov or a Camus. The God who reveals himself in the abandonment of Christ is not a "cold heavenly power" and does not "hover above corpses" but, Moltmann continues, is "known as the human God in the crucified Son of Man" (p. 266), a God who completely assumes the "why?" of man, a God even capable of communicating an entirely other existence beyond Good Friday on Easter morning.

More generally, in his abandonment Jesus is probably the God of our period in a special way, a period in which wars, concentration camps, totalitarian ideologies, and so many other factors seem to cry out everywhere that God is dead. Perhaps never so much as today has the silence of God become so acute, perceptible by human consciousness, and man been so in search of his God. More than ever, the man of today can identify with the face of Christ on the cross, abandoned by his God.

In an article published in "Concilium," Christian Duquoc begins by enumerating the sufferings of the modern world: "monotonous work, unbearable rhythms, limited horizons, anguish and misery of the slums, exploitation, mystification, and violence. . . . Our societies with their high standards of living, even when physical evils are attentuated and concrete insecurities eliminated, generate no less fearful and destructive individual and social pathologies. There is a long train of human suffering, a way of the cross without end: a Good Friday on which the sun never sets, an image of the Crucified that gathers up the misery of the world and projects it in a cry before God: 'Why have you abandoned me?' "[11]

The experience of contemporary humanity is such that only the reality of the abandonment experienced by Christ on the cross, understood as a reality integrated into the Mystery of divine Love, can "justify" a discourse on the existence of a God opened to humanity and give a response to the "why's" of the present times. According to an important thought of E. Schweizer: "In this cry the reality of God is held fast for all times, even for those in which neither experience nor thought could grasp it."[12]

In a suggestive theological meditation entitled "Perspectives,"[13] H. Schürmann enumerates some of the anxieties inherent to the future that assault the humanity of today: "The hour no longer seems very distant when humanity will no longer bear *the lack of metaphysical orientation* and the void into which the question of meaning flows. The 'eclipse of God' (M. Buber), the 'loss of God' (Pascal), the 'death of God' (an expression that from Luther passes through Hegel and resounds until Nietzsche and our days when it has become a slogan), the 'lack of God' (Heidegger), his 'absence': here is a phenomenon that rarefies ever more the atmosphere that the spirit of man needs in order to breathe. The desacralized world, which has become opaque but in return is dominated by tyranical idols and demoniacal material imperatives, is becoming an environment where it is no longer possible to lead a life that is worthy of man" (p. 161).

In particular, this exegete sees in the abandonment of Jesus the solution that can illuminate humanity. For it is the greatest revelation of God's existence for man, i.e., of God's being directed toward the well-being of man: "Jesus is the 'truly' free man, free from himself and from all that hampers his existence. Thus, he is the way in which God exists for humanity and for the cosmos. Only because God has 'irrupted' in Jesus, because he has become present in him at the cost of a surprising 'descent,' and because he dwells in him in love is there an existence of God for man in the existence of Jesus for us; only for this reason do we find in the *engagement* of Jesus that of God" (p. 167).[14]

Outside the field of theology proper, it is worthwhile to point out the interest given by some philosophers of the present generation to our topic. I am thinking, for example, of the book by Philippe Nemo, *Job et l'excès du mal* (Paris, 1978) and in particular of that by Gaspare Mura, *Da Kierkegaard a Moltmann, Giobbe e la "sofferenza di Dio"* (Rome: Città Nuova, 1982).

These thinkers confront a problem that is so acute in our times: anxiety in its various forms of existential anxiety, excess of evil, religious anxiety of sin, etc.

G. Mura analyzes the theme as it has been developed in thinkers like S. Kierkegaard, E. Bloch, E. Stein, P. Tillich, J. Maritain, and J. Moltmann, without forgetting Ph. Nemo and the psychoanalysis of C. G. Jung. The Book of Job is interrogated with great intensity: what response can it give to modern man's problem of anxiety?

Mura, however, does not stop at the phenomenology of anxiety in the Book of Job. He opens it onto the situation of other biblical texts, in particular Psalm 22, the psalm of anxiety and abandonment *par excellence*. The latter reveals "existential situations and connotations of anxiety particularly close to those of Job" (p. 161).

Above all, he notes the connection between Job and the cry of abandonment of Christ on the cross seen as the realization of the "response" to Job. The author asks himself: "Is it possible, beginning with the existential dimension of Job's anxiety, to understand it as a figure of a reality that is hidden in God and in which God himself would be involved?" (p. 158).

Beginning with the reproach that God addresses to Job's interlocutors: "You have not spoken rightly concerning me, as has my servant Job" (Job 42:7), Mura develops this reflection: "Why not think that in the light of these words Job found himself again in the 'meaning' that God attributed to his anxiety and, having glimpsed the mystery, became silent?" (p. 158).

The silence of Job thus opens onto the cry of the Crucified: "Innocent anxiety is the original existential dimension that the

Word assumed at the incarnation and into which from the beginning he inserted his human relationship to the Father, but in which he also lived his 'terminal' abandonment to the Father in the historical condition of the representative of a sinful humanity" (p. 176).

And he concludes: "In the anxiety of God, all human anxiety, all abandonment, and all torment find not only meaning and fulfillment but true redemption" (p. 178).

The validity of these last affirmations is based upon an accurate study carried out by the author:

 • on the nature of anxiety understood not as an accessory but as a reality that is an integral part of the very condition of man;
 • on the possibility of "suffering" in God (where Mura takes advantage of the researches of Maritain, Moltmann . . .).

One can, of course, ask if it is legitimate to put "philosophical" questions to a biblical text. But as a philosopher, G. Mura has known how to respect the sacred text in two ways: he has taken account of the results of exegesis, and he has recognized the limits within which his own thought was able to move. That confirms the validity of his study.

The Abandonment of Christ, Measure and Source of Christian Love

When Jesus suffered the abandonment, when the people mocked the impotence of the Crucified who was unable to save himself, God was totally on the side of the One condemned to the cross, revealed himself in a definitive way, and manifested his love for man, a love that appeared to be weakness, silence, and impotence. But, by refusing a decisive, powerful intervention, God avoids the task of filling the voids of human ignorance and weakness which man would like to assign him. By refusing miraculous and spectacular solutions, God assigns man himself the task of going where there is abandonment, division, atheism, and absence of God in order to fill this negativity with his presence.

The exhortation of the author of the Letter to the Hebrews is along these lines: "Therefore Jesus died outside the gate, to sanctify the people by his own blood. *Let us go* to him outside the camp, bearing the insult which he bore" (Heb 13:12–13).

It is necessary to go out to the crucified Christ who "consecrated" himself outside the Holy City, outside the sphere consecrated to God and reserved for the religious man. One must therefore *dare* to leave the sacred where one feels secure in order to find Christ among the impious, among those without God, for it is there that God has decided to pitch his tent.

Before a society that proclaims the death of God or continually experiences his absence, Christian love must measure itself by that of Christ lived to the point of abandonment, if it wishes to be credible. It must have the courage of Paul who "to those not subject to the law became like one not subject to it," precisely because his law was that of Christ and of him crucified (cf. 1 Cor 9:19ff; 2:2). It is the courage therefore of a love capable of overcoming the barriers of the sacred, of everything that could hinder its universality, its approach to every man. It is a love capable of losing God for God, which means knowing how to recognize him at every moment where one was not seeking him. This implies the courage of knowing how to lose one's own certainty of "possessing him" in order to make a space for one's brother and to find him there. Only a love in conformity with that lived by Christ in the abandonment can be a faithful testimony in the contemporary world of the love of God which in the abandonment of Jesus revealed itself as near to all men in their estrangement from God.

I should like to return to the hymn cited by Paul in the Letter to the Philippians. It speaks of Christ who "though he was in the form of God . . . emptied himself . . . obediently accepting even death, death on a cross!" (Phil 2:6–8).

The exegetes generally consider the final expression "death on a cross" as a clarification proceeding from the hand of the apostle, and perhaps rightly so.

We now know how central the fact is for the theology of Paul that Jesus, the Son sent by God, died on a cross, i.e., on the wood of the curse. He insists on how important it is for the Christian faith to base itself precisely on that which is a scandal for the Jews and foolishness for the others, whereas in Christ, nailed to the wood of the curse, the power and the wisdom of God is manifest (cf. 1 Cor 1:20ff; Gal 3:13).

If, therefore, Paul adds the clarification "death on a cross," the entire hymn is influenced by it and receives a typically Pauline coloring. It is not, in effect, a marginal annotation. On the contrary, the addition comes to occupy a key position and casts a new light precisely on the quality and the value of the obedience lived by Christ: a love precisely such as to become a "curse" for us, as to be made "sin" without being a sinner.

This addition, however, becomes all the more significant through the fact that it is made by the apostle in a hortatory context exhorting us to unity (cf. Phil 2:2–5). It amazes me that in the various commentaries the fact is not better brought to light that precisely in exhorting the community to the life of unity Paul does not present so much as a model the obedience lived by Jesus in general but places the accent on his obedience to the point of death *on the cross*.

Without a doubt, only in a love similar to that lived by Christ on the cross—in the sense in which he understands the cross—does Paul see the key to "all being one," the possibility of overcoming every sort of inability to communicate which afflicts relationships even among members of the same community, the possibility above all that the community may be the body of Christ, and that means the "visible" presence of the Risen One in the world.

J. Guillet (art. cit., 89–90) writes: "Our inability to reach one another, the inability of the mother to console her child who is suffering, the inability of friendship to prevent misunderstandings and divisions, the inability of love to prolong communion and to abolish distances, the loneliness in which we are locked up, the suffering of a tortured humanity—Jesus lives all this in his agony, not from the outside as if he were a saddened witness, but from the inside and in the greatest depths, as the loneliest and most abandoned of all. From the depths of this loneliness, Jesus

Christ can at last gather into unity the dispersed sons of God (Jn 11:52). . . . He can reach us all and reunite us."

If, therefore, in the risen Jesus recreated humanity can be one in God, this is because he in his love of abandonment has drawn close to every man in his loneliness and in his estrangement from God and others. From the writings of J. Guillet one can also deduce that only a love that is similar to the love of Christ in his abandonment and that finds its strength therein is the true foundation of every strong and permanent bond—be it of friendship, between spouses, or in the family.

In his abandonment, Jesus is therefore not only the measure of Christian love with regard to the present world, where God appears to be absent, but also the model of the agape required among the members of the Christian community itself—and by "community" I understand also a family or two or three gathered in the name of Christ (cf. Mt 18:20)—if such a community wishes to realize its vocation: the life of unity.

Only conformity to Christ, particularly to his love of abandonment, only a love ready to lose God for the sake of God, can realize in the believer and in the community that "tear"—to take up again the symbolism of the torn veil which Mark applies precisely to the dying Jesus—which elevates one to the life of God, which makes the divine presence of the Risen One arise, who is the bearer and witness of the love of God for all humanity, and which unites hearts while fostering diversity.

From a theological point of view, this aspect will have to be examined more closely.[15] If in fact the abandonment, as an experience that directly regards the relationship of Christ with his Father, is a revelation of God (see the concluding chapter), this same abandonment in relation to the humanity for which Jesus died—i.e., in the perspective of the redemption—manifests his loss of God as a gift of his bond with the Father, which the Crucified gives to men estranged from God.

In the Christian experience, that means that the reality of the abandonment of Christ is an essential aspect of Christian love: it makes of this love the sacrament of the unifying Spirit. Reciprocal love, lived according to the measure of the abandoned Jesus, permits the Spirit not only to unite persons in Christ but also to make of this unity the reflection of the trinitarian life for the world.

Notes

1. Obviously, the salvific value of the death of Jesus—and thus of the cry of abandonment—would be unthinkable without the resurrection: "The resurrection forms, so to speak, the divine and deep side of the reality of the cross where God definitively comes to man and man definitively comes to God" (W. Kasper, p. 230).

2. J. Moltmann, op. cit., 181.

3. *L'Au-delà retrouvé*, cit., 96.

4. J. Guillet, "Rejeté des hommes et de Dieu, in *Christus*, no. 13, pp. 99–100. This is an aspect of the Pauline interpretation of the cross— "Christ was made 'sin' for us" (cf. 2 Cor 5:21; Gal 3:13)—that corresponds to the theological value of the cry of abandonment in the Gospels. I therefore do not understand the expression of Paul—"Christ was made 'sin' for us"—according to the juridical concept of the redemption, i.e., as the judgment of God on sin, the punishment that Christ undergoes in our place. I understand it as the penetration of Christ—and thus of God—into the situation of estrangement from God that characterizes the human condition of "sin."

5. K. Rahner, *Zur Theologie des Todes. Mit einem Exkurs über das Martyrium*, Quaestiones disputatae, vol. 2 (Freiburg-Basel-Vienna, 1958), p. 64.

6. "L'uomo che fallisce e il suo Dio," *Concilium* 3 (1976):126.

7. Ibid., 125.

8. J. Guillet, art. cit., 95ff.

9. E. Schillebeeckx, op. cit., 690.

10. Cf. the chapter "Kreuzestheologie und Atheismus," pp. 205–214.

11. "Croce del Cristo e sofferenze umana," *Concilium* 9 (1976): 122f.

The author has developed his thought on the abandonment of Christ in his *Christologie*, cit., 39–51. For Duquoc, it is necessary to distinguish three stages of dereliction: "The failure of a work, the anguish of the just man, and the estrangement from God or his abandonment. The third moment is to be understood in relation to the other two" (p. 40). Jesus experiences the failure of his work as the failure of the promises of the beatitudes: the violent continue to dominate the poor. "The suffering of Jesus is not only his own. It is that of all those who have hoped in his word. The failure of his preaching, his condemnation, and death testify that the just man has no support since God does not vindicate his rights" (p. 43).

12. Cited by A. Pronzato, *La passione di Cristo,* op. cit., 126.

13. Published in French in the volume *Comment Jésus a-t-il vécu sa mort?,* Lectio divina, no. 93 (Paris: Cerf, 1977), 145–184.

14. The same exegete makes a similar argument with regard to the situation of the Church also: "There is not only the abandonment of Jesus on the cross where we encounter the darkness of God. This darkness can also envelop entire periods in the history of the Church. There is, however, no doubt that this is to a large degree the situation of the Church today, of our communities, and of many believers who live in the night of the senses and of the spirit. The situation of the Church today is similar to that which is described in 1 Kings 8:11f when Solomon wished to dedicate the recently constructed temple: ' . . . the priests could no longer minister because of the cloud, since the Lord's glory had filled the temple of the Lord. Then Solomon said, "The Lord intends to dwell in the dark cloud." ' . . . When the desolation of the Church and our own darkness are experienced as a participation in the abandonment of the Lord, God will make seeds sprout up from the dark earth that tomorrow will grow and bear blossoms. When God extinguishes the light in the house of the Church it is only because he wishes in the darkness to renovate the furnishings of the house and to modernize it in view of the future. It is necessary to accept the darkness and to bear it as a participation in the abandonment of Jesus" (pp. 180–181).

15. With regard to the theological study of the cry of abandonment, Moltmann's book, *Der gekreuzigte Gott,* is certainly capable of opening the debate in this field. I should furthermore like to point out the excellent theological study that Piero Coda has published in the review *Nuova umanità* (Rome: Città Nuova) on "Gésu crocifisso e abbandonato e la Trinità" [IV:21 (1982); V:24–25 (1983); V:28–29 (1983)].

CHAPTER 8

The Abandonment of Jesus, the Climax of God's Revelation

By way of conclusion, I can only briefly handle this theme which contemporary theology is beginning to explore and which would obviously merit a more ample treatment.

Since in its focal point the abandonment of Jesus is "the desire for the very presence of God," it reveals itself essentially as a story of love between Jesus and his God. The unity—lived as obedience—that bound the person of Christ to the Father in a unique and permanent way and constituted him in his sonship is carried to the point of paradox in the cry of abandonment. We stand before an event that involves God in the "first person," that is comprehensible only as a Father-Son relationship, and that culminates the climax of the revelation of God.

The Revelation of God as Love

"If, however, God reveals himself in the life and death of Jesus (and in his resurrection), the question arises: who is this God who reveals himself to us in Jesus and shows himself as existing for us and sympathizing with us, and how is he in himself?"[1]

Before the abandonment of Christ on the cross—the Christ whom God then raises up—this question arises spontaneously and urgently. The response can only be a revelation of God that upsets our habitual notions. In his book *Il mistero della sofferenza di Dio*, Jean Galot makes it explicit in these terms:

129

On the cross the Son of God experienced the depths of human misery; he had the experience of suffering more than any other man.

One should recognize here the vertex of God's revelation. In the human life of Jesus, everything is a revelation of God. But suffering is the most intense human experience. It is therefore the most effective in demonstrating what God is. It not only indicates the extreme point of the solidarity with humanity assumed by the Word but also manifests his divine face. Even though it remains the suffering of the human nature of Christ, it lets us discover an essential aspect of divine love, its most mysterious aspect in which God appears entirely other to us, entirely different from our human notions. Indeed, the fact that he who is omnipotent is subject to pain is unsettling to us. Here there appears the value of a theological method that does not consist in positing a determinate notion of God and in contesting the reality of everything in Scripture that is not in conformity with it but in fully accepting revelation with an image of God that transcends and overturns our concepts. One cannot begin from the idea of omnipotence, the principle of which excludes every possibility of suffering. The true point of departure lies in the fact that the Omnipotent did suffer. Above all, it draws attention to the primacy of God's love. Omnipotence is not the first absolute attribute that determines in a sovereign way the limits of love. Love is primary, and the divine power is that of love. For this reason, such power is capable of abasing itself to the ultimate depths of suffering. . . .

The pain of the passion lets us have some intuition of the unlimitedness of divine love. This love did not accept the limits that could have been placed by the claims of power and dignity. In his human existence, the Son of God did not claim to be the Untouchable, withdrawn from the vicissitudes of human emotions and feelings, whom suffering would not have affected. On the contrary, he offered himself to human pain without limits and experienced it without reserve because his love wished to go to the end (op. cit., 45f).

Thus, the key to understanding the divine attributes such as omnipotence is love. It is with this latter that one must begin in order to understand something of God's action and of his inner being. But, in turn, it is the crucified Jesus, particularly the reality of the abandonment, that reveals what the omnipotence of divine Love is: the capacity of humbling oneself, of abasing oneself in the human condition to the point of being made "sin." In order to draw near to men estranged from God, God does not fear reaching them in their estrangement, thus appearing as the opposite of God. The traditional image that man had made himself of God—a powerful, glorious, victorious God—is completely overturned here because God here identifies himself with weakness, poverty, and abandonment, and in doing so demonstrates his power. The power of love does not consist in affirming oneself but in giving oneself. It thus distinguishes itself clearly from the idea of domineering and egocentric power which man forms of such an attribute.

This divine power which is love in the abandonment of Jesus involves not only the Son but also the Father: "When Jesus complains of being abandoned, the Father also abandons himself through his silence (i.e., he exposes himself to misunderstanding): he delivers himself to the derision of those who triumphantly exult in being in the right against him and deny him. He sacrifices his power which is his divinity (the ancients defined *divinitas* by *potestas* in the concrete sense of *dominatio*), he identifies himself with the one who suffers and dies," writes J. Moingt in an interesting article published in 1977.[2]

In the One nailed to the cross and repudiated by impotent society, God humiliates himself out of love to the point of "losing face" before men. The accusation and scorn addressed to the Crucified by the various religious categories of the age—a scandal for the Jews, weakness for the Greeks—are in reality addressed directly to God: he appears to man as scandalous and impotent. Again J. Moingt: "By refusing to intervene on Calvary, the Father renounces his power, exposes himself to our misunderstanding, and destroys the advantageous representations we had of him.

And this denudation accomplishes the sovereign act of his freedom in total respect of our freedom. In the entire measure that being known pertains to the being of God, the Father withdraws from our knowledge. He withdraws in a single act of knowledge, that expressed to him by the dying, abandoned Christ" (p. 333). In more simple terms: God discards every purely human mode of knowing God and recognizes as valid only that which passes through the abandoned Jesus.

In reality, then, God is "never greater than in this humiliation. He is never more glorious than in this self-surrender. He is never more powerful than in this impotence. God is never more divine than in this humanity." In the cross of Jesus, God is "love with his whole being."[3]

The weakness of God is the manifestation of his power because it is love, an unlimited love capable of humbling itself.

"As Love, God is so much self-surrender that, 'emptying' himself, he can 'descend' (cf. Phil 2:6ff) to the incarnation, even to death and to the hell of our sins, where the Father 'delivers' (*dahingibt*) the Son to abandonment by God, and the latter from out of his abandonment by God 'surrenders' (*hingibt*) himself to God."[4]

In a note, H. Schürmann cites W. Kasper: "Only on the cross is the being of God revealed to us at its deepest roots, i.e., this absolute freedom without boundaries, freedom to the point of self-denudation in order to become the contrary of what God appears to be, freedom to the point of death."

In the abandonment, God reveals himself in a definitive way as love, and at the same time unveils what love is.

Revelation of Intratrinitarian Life

The crucified and abandoned Jesus not only manifests to the full who God is in regard to us; the event lived on the cross also opens onto the mystery of the inner life of God.

Meditation on the Gospel and putting it into practice, without which there is no effective knowledge, let us discover that in the depths of Jesus there dwells the presence of Another whom he calls his Father and that he (Jesus) constitutes his own personal being in virtue of his filial relationship to the Father to the point of expressing it on the cross, casting himself into the Other in an act of total dispossession and of total giving of himself to the other.

Meditation on the passion and its practice lets us understand the reciprocity that is effected between the Father and Christ. The extremes of abandonment to which this perfect servant of God is reduced reveal as its *raison d'être* another abandonment, that of the Father who delivers himself to us in the One whom he delivers to us. . . . [5]

On the same page, J. Moingt affirms that the abandonment of Jesus is the highest and most definitive manifestation of the love lived in the bosom of the Trinity. It is thus necessary to understand the non-intervention of God positively as the culminating expression of the Father's love for the Son:

When interrogated in the light of Easter, the scandalous silence of God on Calvary becomes revelation. God manifests himself by disappearing in death of Christ. He manifests himself as the interiority of this event of death . . . as the exchange of relationships and of gifts that constitute them, the one and the other, in their being of Father and Son.

The Father reveals himself on the cross not despite his silence and his non-intervention but positively, by contrast, in this silence and through the very fact of abandoning his Son. He intervenes insofar as he abstains from intervening, and this abstention is a decisive and definitive act. . . .

From this text of Moingt, there appears the necessity of reading the Calvary event from a trinitarian perspective: "Only the trinitarian mystery permits one to understand the profound theological meaning of the cross. It alone permits us to make of the cross not only an event, an ordinary chronicle fact of this world, or the unjust death of an innocent man, but a 'theological' reality, a reality that regards God," writes P. Ferlay with good reason,[6] who takes up and develops his thought a few pages later:

> The light of the trinitarian mystery illuminates the cross of Jesus. If God is not a trinitarian mystery, the cross is a fact of this world. It is the pious death of a just man, and at the most it will be able to express the solidarity of this man with the oppressed. All those who think that the trinitarian affirmation is not essential to the faith are unable to give to the cross its value as a revelation of God. The trinitarian mystery gives the reality of the cross its meaning. . . . We who know that God is the exchange of love in the self-giving of the persons understand the attitude of Christ on the cross. During his life, Jesus called himself "meek and humble" (Mt 11:29). But how are we to know whether these appellatives surpass his humanity? In order to know this, the trinitarian revelation is necessary.
>
> It is not only Jesus of Nazareth who is meek and humble, but also the Father, Son, and Spirit who give themselves to one another, forgetting themselves. The Christian God will never reveal himself in power because it is not in power that he lives his inner mystery but, on the contrary, in the gift of self, in submission, and in what we might be tempted to call a certain poverty. The meekness of Christ on the cross, his humility, and his radical poverty are manifest and comprehensible thanks solely to the trinitarian mystery (p. 936).

As Ferlay affirms, the trinitarian revelation lets us understand that the humility and meekness of Jesus are not only a virtue of the Jesus of history but a reflection, a transparency of the trinitarian relationships which appear at their highest point on the cross.

In Jesus the relationship existing within the Trinity between the Son and the Father acquires a historical countenance; it becomes, so to speak, visible.

In his death (and already during his life), Christ experiences as man what he lives eternally as Son of God in the Trinity, i.e., his complete dependence with regard to the Father in love. There obviously exists a very deep hidden bond between the denudation of Calvary and the gift that Christ makes of himself through the redemptive incarnation, on the one hand, and, on the other, the perfect gift that the divine persons make of themselves in the trinitarian life, each one of them being himself insofar as given.[7]

In this perspective, the abandonment of Jesus on the cross appears then as the manifestation of love in its pure state: it is the personified definition of love which by its very nature is when it is not, i.e., when it gives itself, when it is Relationship.[8]

But this love which unites the Son and the Father reveals itself in the particular form it takes when it is lived completely in the condition of sinful humanity and consequently experienced as the greatest of torments. G. Mura synthesizes it well: "In the abandonment, Christ has in reality performed the same act of abandonment to the Father that he eternally performs within the divinity: Verbum spirans amorem. But he has lived it out under the historical conditions of human anguish with its burden of sin and torment."[9]

I shall now address this question in a synthetic way in order to take into consideration the various opinions of the exegetes.

What, then, took place in the abandonment between Jesus and his God?

If in that event Jesus became conscious of the reality of sin in all its crudeness as loss of God and thus felt the weight of the divine "anger," of God's categorical "no" to the evil that slays man, does that not imply a real separation between Christ and the Father?

C. E. B. Cranfield, for example, thinks this: "The burden of the world's sin, his complete self-identification with sinners, involved not merely a felt, but a real abandonment by his Father. It is in the cry of dereliction that the full horror of man's sins stands revealed." In parentheses the author specifies: "It is, of course, theologically important to maintain the paradox that, while this God-forsakenness was utterly real, the unity of the Blessed Trinity was even then unbroken."[10]

This paradox does not end in a pure contradiction because the author's reasoning bears in mind the reality of the "two natures" of Christ. What takes place in Jesus does not disturb the unity of the intratrinitarian life. But all this appears very abstract.

J. Moltmann also affirms a true separation on account of the death of the curse but does so in a more radical way since, going beyond the "two natures" view, he places himself directly on the plain of intratrinitarian relationships: the Father rejects the Son; and, at the same time, there is a true unity on account of their self-giving.[11]

There persists in these theologians a fidelity to the Lutheran thought of the "crucified God" who undergoes our curse.

But one remains perplexed before the affirmation of a real separation in God between the divine persons. Moltmann gives the impression of placing the state of the human condition directly into the being of God. How is one to justify this enterprise theologically?

Catholic theologians prefer to see in the abandonment the extreme manifestation—according to the possibilities of the human condition—of the qualities of love between the divine persons. In the abandonment of Christ, the total love of the Father for the Son becomes visible and vice versa, a love such that the persons exist as a full gift of self and receive themselves as a gift of the one to the other.

In reality, the absence of God experienced in the abandonment characterizes the loving presence of the Father who gives to Christ the possibility of being fully himself as Son—just as the abandonment experienced by the Son allows the Father to be such. In short, the specific dynamism of love is verified in all its profundity.

If the Father had intervened before the death, if he had interrupted the experience of abandonment with an act of power before it was fully finished, an abandonment which for Jesus meant complete, unlimited gift of himself, he would have limited the love of Jesus for him, he would not have allowed him to express his filial relationship, his being Son, to the full. But by this very fact, he would not have been fully Father. In a certain sense, Jesus "generates" the Father in the abandonment.

Therefore, there is not a real separation between the divine persons but a life of unity such as to lead to full distinction: "The death of Christ is the moment that makes the distinction between the Father and the Son appear more sharply. The unity seems to be ruptured. To speak in familiar terms, one would not have believed that the Father and the Son within the mystery of the one God were so distinct that the one would have been capable of going so far from the other out of love."[12]

"But at that moment unity prevails, and this unity is the Spirit. The death of Christ reveals that the bond of love between the Father and the Son is stronger than all the forces of dispersion. The Spirit is this bond of love. . . . The hour of the cross is thus the privileged revelation of the trinitarian mystery as the mystery of perfect charity and gift of self."[13]

This interpretation certainly possesses great value, but does it go to the bottom of the question? Does not the abandonment also imply a "newness" in God himself? The reflections of J. Moingt point in this direction (p. 330):

It is not enough to say that the God of Jesus Christ is a new God insofar as he is to be known neither after the manner of the Jews nor after that of the Greeks, locked up neither in the religious categories of Judaism nor in the definitions of philosophy. His newness is also in him and not only on our part. If it is true, as we have said, that the manifestation of God belongs to his being, then one can, indeed one must understand that he has *become* new in himself by means of the historical act of revealing himself in time, in man, in passion and death, and in the open future with the resurrection.[14]

One thus arrives at the question: Is Jesus' experience of the abandonment the highest point of trinitarian revelation, or does it also entail a "newness," does it constitute an event within the Trinity itself?

Does the abandonment involve the incarnate Son without at the same time affecting his intratrinitarian relationships? When Jesus dies on the cross and cries out his abandonment, does the immanent Trinity—in its relationships *ad intra*—remain uninvolved?[15]

Moltmann's question is legitimate: "*To what degree* was God affected by the death of Jesus? For this death should affect him in his very heart and not only in an external relation."[16]

If—the theologian continues—God is not only in Christ but Christ is God, then one cannot only speak of "God in the crucified"; one must speak of "God on the cross."

"If one takes this seriously, one must . . . say further that what happened on the cross was an event between God and God. . . . "[17]

I am in doubt, however, about Moltmann's conclusion which transposes the experience of the abandonment of Jesus into the Trinity and consequently affirms that God enters into conflict with God.

In any case, I shall conclude with two observations:

• The alternative of abandonment as culminating revelation of the trinitarian life or as "newness" in God should not be understood in an exclusive way, i.e., in such a way as to think that the one truth is incompatible with the other. The revelation of intratrinitarian life means the revelation of the permanent newness that characterizes such a life in God.

• If the abandonment constitutes an event in God himself, this event does not take place—according to the image we commonly form of the Trinity—in a "closed circle in heaven" (K. Barth) but opens onto earth and involves it also. Man enters into that event between God and God. The incarnation no longer allows us to consider an intratrinitarian event in abstraction from the total—hence human—reality of the Son of God.

Notes

1. Schürmann, *Jesu ureigener Tod. Exegetische Besinnungen und Ausblicke* (Freiburg-Basel-Vienna), 143.

2. "Montre-nous le Père," *Recherches de science religieuse* 2 (1977):325.

3. J. Moltmann, op. cit., 190.

4. H. Schürmann, op. cit., 144f.

5. Moingt, op. cit., 324.

6. P. 934. Moltmann also: "In order to understand what happened between Jesus and his God and Father on the cross, one has to speak in a trinitarian fashion" (p. 230).

7. A. Feuillet, *L'Agonie de Gethsémani* (Paris: Gabalda, 1977), 260.

8. The abandonment, then, reveals to a maximum degree the being of God: Love. One understands what an upset such a fact must have been for the common mentality, for philosophy, and even for the very behavior of those who were already "following Christ."

Schürmann writes, citing Kasper: "Christian faith defines the meaning of being as love. . . . That means an unimaginably radical transvaluation of the whole of ancient metaphysics. The substance resting and existing in itself is no longer the highest but that which for Aristotle was the weakest: relationship, being for another, self-bestowing love" (p. 144).

In a note, Schürmann takes up and modulates this reflection, again citing Kasper: "To proclaim that God is love, i.e., that love is the ultimate sense of all reality. . . . This conception of reality held by Christianity represents a revolution such that it is difficult to imagine a greater one. The supreme perfection is no longer, as in Greek metaphysics, that of the self-contained and self-sufficient substance but being for others and with others. There follows a revolution in our way of understanding God: God is no longer the unmoved mover but he who of his very nature is life and love and who can therefore be the God of men and the God of history."

Concretely, it follows that love lived to the point of abandonment—which constitutes the maximum revelation of the being of God—can and must become the criterion of behavior for the believer if such behavior is to be in harmony with the being of God and thus with his will. And this love manifests itself as the possibility of total self-denudation, of losing, for example, what could be considered as "inspirations" when it is a question of listening to the other, of welcoming his thought, etc. The penetration of the life of God into the human takes place, as with Jesus, in the nothingness of love that manifests his abandonment. It is in this sense, as we have seen, that the understanding of the torn veil is oriented in Mark 15:38.

9. "L'angoscia innocente IV," *Nuova umanità* 14 (1981):56.

10. *The Gospel According to St. Mark,* The Cambridge Greek Testament Commentary (Cambridge, 1966), 458–459.

11. Op. cit., 282–291.

12. Shortly thereafter the author specifies: "The Son stands before the Father, distinct from him to the point of being able to say to him: 'My God, why have you abandoned me?' "

13. P. Ferlay, art. cit., pp. 937–938.

14. The theologian continues: "To admit that newness is intrinsic to God is to place God in the process of becoming or to place a certain form of temporality in him. This idea is one of the most recent and most revolutionary acquisitions of theology owing to a great extent to the fecundity of Hegelian thought. Needless to say, it is a difficult notion to employ if one wishes to think the concept of God with rigor, but it does rest on very serious arguments. It is based above all on the refusal to consider what happens in Jesus and on the cross as something external to God; since the Christ event is a world event, this refusal forbids us to place God far from the world and history in order to fix him in immobility and leads one to think of the whole history of the world as the history of salvation and the latter as the history of God.

"Other reasons point in the same direction: life is only movement and tension toward the future. The divine life is essentially freedom, thus self-discovery. It is love which manifests itself in creativity. In God, time is newness without being change or dispersion: it is the space of intersubjective and personal life where the trinitarian relationships of Father, Son, and Spirit are unfolded in such a way that each of the three finds in the other a future that is the new presence of the unfailing past which each one is for the other."

15. "If one understands the death of Jesus solely along the lines of the incarnation, one still remains in the realm of the two natures doctrine. His death remains a human death, even if one accepted by God and thus one that affects God in his turning toward man. The doctrine of the *communicatio idiomatum realis* can then interpret it as a 'death of God,' " as J. Moltmann formulates the classical doctrine in his article "Kreuzestheologie," p. 73.

16. Art. cit., 72.

17. Ibid., 73.

Bibliography

Boman, Th. "Das lezte Wort Jesus." *Studia teologica* 17 (1963):103–119.

Bonhoeffer, D. *Ethique*. Labor et fides. Geneva, 1949.

_____. *Le prix de la grâce*. Ed. Delachaux et Niestlé. Neuchâtel, 1962.

Bultmann, R. *Die Geschichte der synoptischen Tradition*. 7th ed. Göttingen: Vanderhoeck und Ruprecht, 1967.

_____. *Jesus*. Munich and Hamburg: Siebensten Taschenbuch Verlag, 1967.

_____. *Theologie des Neuen Testaments*. 6th ed. Tübingen: J.C.B. Mohr, 1968.

Cranfield, C.E.B. *The Gospel According to St. Mark*. The Cambridge Greek Testament Commentary. C.F.D. Moule, ed. Cambridge, 1966.

Da Spinetoli, O. *Matteo. Commento al "Vangelo della Chiesa"*. 2nd ed. Cittadella ed. Assisi, 1973.

Dauer, A. *Die Passionsgeschichte im Johannesevangelium. Eine traditionsgeschichtliche und theologische Untersuchung zu Joh 18, 1–19. 30*. Munich: Kösel-Verlag, 1972.

Delorme, J. *Lettura del Vangelo de Marco*. Quaderni di spiritualità, vol. 20. Cittadella ed. Assisi, 1977. (Original title: *Lecture de l'Evangile selon saint Marc*. Cahiers evangile, vol. 1/2. Paris: Cerf, 1972).

Del Paramos, S. *Vangelo secondo Matteo*. Nuovo Testamento. Città Nuova ed. Rome, 1970.

Delumeau, J. *Le péché et la peur. La culpabilisation en Occident XIII–XVIII siècles*. Paris: Fayard, 1983.

Diaz, J.A. *Vangelo secondo Marco*. Nuovo Testamento. Città Nuova ed. Rome, 1970.

Dormeyer, D. *Der Sinn des Leidens Jesu. Historisch-kritische und textpragmatische Analysen zur Markuspassion*. Stuttgarter Bibel-Studien, vol. 96. Stuttgart: Verlag Katholisches Bibelwerk GmbH, 1979.

Duquoc, Chr. "Croce del Cristo e sofferenza umana." *Concilium* (Italian edition) 9 (1976):123ff.

_____. *Christologie. Essai dogmatique.* 2 vols. Paris: Cerf, 1972.

Ferlay, P. "Trinité, mort en croix, Eucharistie. Réflexion théologique sur ces trois mystères." *Nouvelle revue théologique* 9 (1974):933ff.

Feuillet, A. *L'Agonie de Gethsémani.* Paris: Gabalda, 1977.

Fromm, E. *Voi sarete come dèi.* Roma, 1970.

Galot, J. *Il mistero della sofferenza di Dio.* Cittadella ed. Assisi, 1975.

George, A. *Etudes sur l'oeuvre de Luc.* Sources bibliques. Paris: Gabalda, 1978.

Gerhardsson, B. "Jésus livré et abandonné d'apres la passion selon Saint Matthieu." *Revue biblique* 2 (1969):206–225.

Gese, H. "Psalm 22 und das Neue Testament." *Zeitschrift für Theologie und Kirche* 68 (1968):1ff.

Gnilka, J. "Mein Gott, mein Gott, warum hast du mich verlassen?" *Biblische Zeitschrift* 3 (1959):294–297.

_____. *Das Evangelium nach Markus.* Evangelisch-katholischer Kommentar zum Neuen Testament. 2 vols. Zurich: Benziger-Neukirchener Verlag, 1978–1979.

Goppelt, L. *Christologie und Ethik. Aufsätze zum Neuen Testament.* Göttingen: Vandenhoeck und Ruprecht, 1968.

Grelot, P. *Dans les angoisses l'espérance. Enquête biblique.* Paris: Edition du Seuil, 1983.

Guillet, J. "Rejeté des hommes et de Dieu." *Christus,* no. 13, pp. 83–100.

_____. *Jésus devant sa vie et sa mort.* Paris: Aubier, 1971.

Hengel, M. *La crucifixion.* Lectio divina, vol. 105. Paris: Cerf, 1981. (Original title: "Mors turpissima crucis. Die Kreuzigung in der antiken Welt und die 'Torheit' des 'Wortes vom Kreuz.'" *Rechtfertigung. Festschrift für E. Käsemann.* Tübingen, 1976, pp. 125–184).

Hermann, I. *Das Markusevangelium.* Düsseldorf: Patmos, 1965.

Jeremias, J. *Die Verkündigung Jesu. Neutestamentliche Theologie.* Vol. I. Gütersloh: Gerd Mohn, 1971.

Käsemann, E. *Exegetische Versuche und Besinnungen.* Vol. I. 4th ed. Göttingen: Vandenhoeck und Ruprecht, 1965.

Kasper, W. *Jesus der Christus.* Mainz: Matthias-Grünewald Verlag, 1974.

Kierkegaard, S. *Diario 1854.* Vol. II. Brescia, 1963.

Lagrange, M.-J. *Evangile selon Saint-Marc.* Etudes bibliques. Paris: Gabalda, (1929) 1966.

Lamarche, P. "Révélation de Dieu chez Marc." *Le point théologique,* vol. 20. Paris: Beauchesne, 1976.

Léon-Dufour, X. *Face à la mort. Jésus et Paul.* Paris: Edition du Seuil, 1979.

Linnemann, E. *Studien zur Passionsgeschichte.* Forschungen zur Religion und Literatur des Alten und Neuen Testaments, vol. 102. Göttingen, 1970.

Lohse, E. *Die Geschichte des Leidens und Sterbens Jesu Christi.* Gütersloh: Gerd Mohn, 1964.

Mann, D. *Mein Gott, mein Gott, warum hast du mich verlassen? Eine Auslegung der Passionsgeschichte nach Markus.* Neukirchen-Vluyn, 1980.

Martelet, G. *L'Au-delà retrouvé. Christologie des fins dernières.* Paris: Desclée, 1975.

Merklein, H. and Zenger, E., eds. *Ich will euer Gott werden.* Stuttgarter Bibel-Studien, vol. 100. Stuttgart, 1981.

Minnette de Tillesse, G. *Le secret messianique dans l'évangile de Marc.* Lectio divina, vol. 47. Paris: Cerf, 1968.

Moingt, J. "Montre-nous le Père." *Recherches de science religieuse* 2 (1977):305ff.

Moltmann, J. *Der gekreuzigte Gott.* Munich: Kaiser Verlag, 1972.

————. *Zukunft der Schöpfung. Gesammelte Aufsätze.* Munich: Kaiser Verlag, 1977.

Mura, G. "L'angoscia innocente, IV." *Nuova umanità* 14 (1981):7–58.

————. *Da Kierkegaard a Moltmann, Giobbe e la "sofferenza di Dio".* Rome: Città Nuova, 1982.

Mussner, Fr. *Praesentia salutis. Gesammelte Studien zu Fragen und Themen des Neuen Testaments,* Düsseldorf: Patmos, 1967.

Nicolas, M.-J. *Théologie de la résurrection.* Paris: Desclée, 1982.

Pesch, R. *Das Markus-Evangelium.* Herders theologischer Kommentar zum Neuen Testament. 2 vols. Freiburg: Herder, 1976–1977.

Pronzato, A. *La passione di Cristo. Un cristiano comincia a leggere il vangelo di Marco.* Vol. 3. Torino: Gribaudi, 1980.

Rahner, K. *Zur Theologie des Todes. Mit einem Exkurs über das Martyrium.* Quaestiones disputatae, vol. 2. 3rd ed. Freiburg: Herder, 1958.

Rehm, M. "Eli, Eli, lamma sabacthani," *Biblische Zeitschrift* 2 (1958):275–278.

Rupert, L. *Jesus als der leidende Gerechte? Der Weg Jesu im Lichte eines alt- und zwischentestamentlichen Motivs.* Stuttgarter Bibel-Studien, vol. 59. Stuttgart: KBW Verlag, 1972.

Sahlin, H. "Zum Verständnis von drei Stellen des Markus-Evangeliums," *Biblica* 1 (1952):53–63.

Schenke, L. *Der gekreuzigte Christus. Versuch einer literarkritischen Bestimmung der vormarkansichen Passionsgeschichte.* Stuttgarter Bibel-Studien, vol. 69. Stuttgart: KBW Verlag, 1974.

Schillebeeckx, E. *Gesú. La storia di un vivente.* Biblioteca di teologia contemporanea, vol. 26. Brescia: Queriniana, 1976. (Original title: *Jezus, het verhaal van een levende.* Bloemendaal: H. Nelissen, 1974).

Schnackenburg, R. *Das Johannes Evangelium.* 3rd ed. Herders theologischer Kommentar zum Neuen Testament, vol. 3. Freiburg: Herder, 1975.

Schoonenberg, P. "L'uomo che fallisce e il suo Dio." *Concilium* (Italian edition) 3 (1976):118ff.

Schreiber, J. *Die Markuspassion. Wege der Erforschung der Leidensgeschichte Jesu.* Hamburg, 1969.

Schürmann, H. *Jesu ureigener Tod. Exegetische Besinnungen und Ausblicke.* Freiburg, 1975.

Schweitzer, A. *Geschichte der Leben-Jesu-Forschung.* 2nd ed. Tübingen, 1913.

Stauffer, E. "Boao." *Grande lessico del Nuovo Testamento.* Brescia:

Paideia, 1966. II:292ff. (Original title: *Theologisches Wörter-buch zum Neuen Testament*. Stuttgart: Verlag von W. Kohl-hammer, 1933. I:624–627).

Taylor, V. *The Gospel According to St. Mark*. 2nd ed. London: Mac-millan, St. Martin's Press, 1962.

Trilling, W. *Christusverkündigung in den synoptischen Evangelien. Beispiele gattungsgemäßer Auslegung*. Munich: Kösel-Verlag, 1969.

Urs von Balthasar, H. "Mysterium paschale." Feiner, J. and Löhrer, M., eds. *Mysterium salutis*. Vol. III/2. Einsiedeln: Benziger Ver-lag, 1969.

———. *Herrlichkeit—Theologie: Neuer Bund*. Vol. III/2. Einsie-deln: Johannes Verlag, 1969.

Vanhoye, A. "Structure et théologie des récits de la passion dans les évangiles synoptiques." *Nouvelle revue théologique* 2 (1967):135ff.

Weber, H.-R. *Kreuz. Überlieferung und Deutung der Kreuzigung Jesu im neutestamentlichen Kulturraum*. Stuttgart, 1975.